And I Heard Him Whisper...

Hearing the voice of God!
A devotional of heavenly whispers.

Marcy Mikolajewski

Copyright 2024 – Marcy Mikolajewski

All rights reserved. No part of this publication may be reproduced, distributed, or transmitted in any form or by any means, including photocopying, recording, or other electronic or mechanical methods, without the prior written permission of the publisher, except in the case of brief quotations embodied in critical reviews and certain other non-commercial uses permitted by copyright law.

All Scripture quotations, unless otherwise indicated, are taken from The New Living Translation (NLT) Tyndale House Publisher, the English Standard Version (ESV) Crossway Publisher, The Passion Translation (TPT) BroadStreet Publishing Group LLC, The Message (MSG) NavPress Publishing Group, The Amplified Bible Classic Edition (AMPC) The Lockman Foundation, or the King James Version (KJV).

Printed in the United States of America.

ISBN: 979-8-3485-6212-0

10 9 8 7 6 5 4 3 2 1

EMPIRE PUBLISHING
www.empirebookpublishing.com

I dedicate this book to the "new harvest people", all those who come to know Jesus in this new era. Those longing to hear God's voice as they seek to follow Him.

This book is also for the seasoned follower of Jesus, who simply loves to hear from the heart of God.

Table of Contents

Section 1: Journey Into His Heart 7
    He said, "Write It Down" 8
    "Lord, help me make a difference." 10
    Dragon Slayer! 12
    Open the Treasure Box 14
    Why, God, Why? 16
    Dream With Me 18
    Run With the Wind! 20

Section 2: Under His Wings 23
    Someone Is Watching 24
    Cast Your Cares 26
    Come Out of the Shadows 28
    Give it to Papa 30
    Kid, I've Got You! 32
    The Shaking 34
    My Father's "To Do List" 36

Section 3: Our Father Calls 39
    The Day He Called Me 40
    Step Up to Step Out 42
    It's Morning 44
    Your Prayers Matter! 46
    Exciting Times! 48
    Let The Dominoes Fall 50
    Bring The Fire! 52

Section 4: You Will Know It Is Me 55
The Foot Washing 56
Soar High with Me! 58
A God Encounter 60
Shaken to Awaken! 62
You Carry My Torch! 64
Say The Words 66
Listen Up! 68

Section 5: Immersed in His Presence 71
The Dance 72
Glory Be! 74
"Open" in the Mind of Christ 76
Sitting With the King 78
The "Little Foxes" 80
The Whirlwind! 82
Deep, Deep Joy 84

Section 6: Beautiful In His Eyes 87
Be Beautiful 88
Blessed and Highly Favored 90
What Do You Think? 92
Without Spot or Wrinkle 94
Melt Into His Heart 96
Stand and Shine 98
Ditch the Basket 100

Section 7: I Will Meet You in Your Praise 103

Praise is a Beautiful Thing.. 104
I Will Meet You 106
Sing!... 108
Praise in Your Pain 110
Stand on the Word!... 112
Just Gotta Praise Him!.. 114
Dancing In the Kitchen 116

Section 8: Warriors of the Kingdom 119
Be A Warrior!.. 120
Authority of My Church 122
Forbid Them!.. 124
Stand and Roar!... 126
Scorch Their Tails!... 128
Weirder and Weirder!.. 130
Holy Oil 132

Section 9: Strength In God's Love 135
Keep Moving!... 136
Pray, Wait and Watch 138
Yes, You Are Healed! 140
You Shall Not Go Down!... 142
Armed and Ready for Battle... 144
Walk In the Fire!.. 146
Right Here, Right Now!... 148
Fight the Good Fight!... 150

Section 10: Finding Peace and Joy 153

THE HAPPY PLACE	154
NO PLACE FOR FEAR	156
TAKE IT FOR GRANTED	158
NEEDING TO BE HELD	160
THERE'S A BETTER CHOICE	162
MAINTAIN A GRATEFUL HEART	164
OUR OASIS	166
SECTION 11: RESCUED BY THE KING!	**169**
WARRIOR DOWN	170
IN CLOSING	**175**
THE FUNNY GLASS CLOWN	176
CLOSING PRAYER	179
ABOUT THE AUTHOR	181
CONTACT INFORMATION:	183

Endorsements

I have read many devotional books in my lifetime, but none spoke to me as clearly as "And I Heard Him Whisper". It was like the Holy Spirit was speaking directly to me. I know He gave the message to Marcy, but it was as encouraging and powerful to me as I am sure it was for her! She backs up His words with scripture, which is so important!

God wants to speak to all of us personally if we will stop and take time to listen and write it down. I am guilty of listening to Him but not always writing it down! This book definitely makes you want to take time and do that.

I have known Marcy for years. She has the sweetest spirit!! A girl that I always admired and wished so many times that I was more like. I encouraged Marcy to get this book published fast so I could give it not only to my family but to everyone I know.

Effie Reid,
Entrepreneur and Inspirational Speaker
Belmont, North Carolina

I love this book! This is a book that you will keep going back to many times. As you read, you will come to know the heart of God and His sweet Holy Spirit. This is a much-needed message for today, and I am indeed grateful to my best friend, Marcy, for sharing with us these wonderful messages and stories.

Katie Dziech
Long time friend and sister in Christ

While the world seemed to be shouting and in chaos in March 2020, God was breathing new life into one woman's journey to hearing Him speak above the noise. Through what was described by most as an unprecedented year, it was in the midst of it, that His still, small voice spoke tenderly and "And I Heard Him Whisper" was birthed.

Scripture is clear on the topic of hearing from God, and Marcy has a way with words that beautifully and graciously invites each and every one of us into her living room for an honest and Christ centered conversation about God and hearing him speak.

This book will encourage you and bring a sense of thrill as you encounter His whisper into your own heart.

Jessica Zawalich

Connections and Discipleship Pastor,

The Valley Church, Troy, Ohio

It has been both an honor and blessing to have read this book and have known the author for 50 years!

The loving whispers that God our Father has spoken through her will bring moments of encouragement in His presence with Him.

I pray this book speaks to you as it has spoken to me.

Jan Klosterman

Long time friend and sister in Christ

"The greatest journey I've ever taken was my journey into His Heart.
As He beckoned me, I ventured in.

Standing in His presence, He spoke into my innermost spirit.
His voice was so gentle, like a whisper."

Marcy Mikolajewski

Introduction

My heart has heard you say, "Come and talk with me." And my heart responds, "Lord, I am coming." Psalm 27:8

The God of the universe wants to talk with us. Is that not amazing! It is his desire to forge a relationship with his children. He wants us to know him and how much he loves us. We are precious to him. We are not just any kids; we are <u>HIS</u> kids. What father would not want to talk to his kids?

When a child is in trouble, or hurt, wouldn't a good father comfort that child with soothing words of hope. And when a child is afraid, a good father will always offer words of reassurance.

This is what our Father does for me and will do for you. He is a good, good Father who wants us to know his heart. What better way to get to know someone than through conversation with one another? Prayer is meant for this, but so often our conversation is one-sided. We talk, He listens. It is hard to get to know someone like that.

I love to walk and talk with my Father. In this book, I am sharing some words whispered into my heart that have blessed and comforted me. I hope they will do the same for you. I am nobody special, hearing God's voice is meant for all believers.

Jesus said, *"My sheep hear my voice, and I know them, and they follow me."* (John 10:27). It is pretty clear what Jesus is saying here. As children of God, his "sheep", we should be hearing his voice.

He will speak to us in different ways, through the Bible, through another person, through a song, and sometimes, the Holy Spirit will speak directly into your heart.

When we become a child of God through receiving Jesus as our personal Savior, He comes to live in us and our spirit is joined to

His. Jesus spoke these words *"You will know that I am in my Father, and you are in me, and I am in you."* (John 14:20)

In this same section of scripture, Jesus tells us about the Holy Spirit. Before he died, Jesus said this to his disciples:

> *"But when the Father sends the Advocate as my representative — that is, the Holy Spirit — he will teach you everything and will remind you of everything I have told you."* (John 14:26)

When I received Jesus as my personal Savior, the first thing that I noticed was that the Bible suddenly made sense to me. Not only could I read it with clarity, but I was supernaturally drawn to it. My hunger to learn more about this God of love was insatiable! It was, of course, the Holy Spirit tenderly calling me, guiding me, and teaching me. It was like getting to hear what God was thinking.

> *"No one can know a person's thoughts except that person's own spirit, and no one can know God's thoughts except God's own Spirit. And we have received God's Spirit (not the world's spirit), so we can know the wonderful things God has freely given us."* (1 Corinthians 2: 11-12)

I might state at this point that there is something that we must be aware of. The devil also likes to whisper in our ear. 1 Peter 5:8 warns us, *"Stay alert! Watch out for your great enemy, the devil. He prowls around like a roaring lion, looking for someone to devour."*

Even Jesus warned us, in Luke 21:8, *"Watch out that you are not deceived."* Which tells me, we can be deceived. Remember what happened to Adam and Eve in Genesis Chapter 3.

You might be picturing the old cartoon character with an angel on one shoulder and the devil on the other. Since you can't see the little red devil suit, how do you know who is talking?

Don't worry, you can know the difference between God and the devil. The devil speaks into our carnal mind, but God speaks into the heart, our spirit. Also, God will never go against His written Word and His Word never changes. Most importantly, when God speaks, He speaks love. It will be encouraging, refreshing, and restorative.

It is through the leading of the Holy Spirit into God's Word that I have come to know the heart of the Father. Often a message starts with a scripture that stands out to me. Other times He speaks into my spirit and then confirms the message with scripture. Either way, knowing that there is a "deceiver/devil" lurking about. I always check to make sure that what I am hearing is scriptural and that it follows with what I know is the character of God.

It is not an audible voice that I hear, but an impression deep in my heart and inner-most being that reveals His heart to mine. It took me a while, but once I believed it was His will, I learned to listen. It was no longer just me talking to God, suddenly through my faith in His love and His Word, a two-way communication opened up and my adventure began.

The greatest journey I've ever taken was my journey into His heart. As He beckoned me, I ventured in. Standing in His presence, He spoke into my inner-most spirit. His voice was so gentle, like a whisper.

One of the first things I remember the Lord saying to me kind of blew my mind. I was not expecting him to say what he did. On that particular day I was trying to figure out what I was to do with my life. What was I created for? Now that my kids are raised, what would be my purpose? I turned those feelings into prayer and began to write in my journal what I was hearing in my spirit. He said:

"Child from My heart, I created you to love you. That is your main purpose."

And He continued...

"I have known you for an eternity. I know this is hard for you to understand, but my love is not confined in time. I have always loved you and hoped that you would love me back. My hope was that you would seek me and find me and that you would get acquainted with the heart that you were created from.

Your time on earth is but a journey home. A time for you to find love and purpose and yourself. When you seek to discover who you are and why you were created, seek also to find Me. I have answers for you. I have a wonderful plan for your life. One that will bring you joy and fulfillment.

I am not hard to find, just open your heart and invite me to enter in. Entrust your spirit into my hands for I am a faithful God who loves you. Stay close and I will lead you into your destiny."

This book is a devotional of His heart as whispered into mine. Many of the entries are taken from my weekly blog, **"And I Heard Him Whisper…"** published on WordPress.com. However, as I continue to listen, He continues to speak. In this book I am sharing some of the wonderful insights received through the Holy Spirit during intimate moments with my Father and Jesus.

It is my hope to reveal His heart to you through writing what He has said to me, but truly, I believe <u>He is also speaking to you.</u> I encourage you to read these messages prayerfully and expectantly, listening for what He is saying, into your life.

My hope is that this little book will be found on your nightstand or the front seat of your car. It can be read through as a daily devotional, but I've also designed it so that you can pick it up and read any page and be blessed by the heart of God. I pray the Holy Spirit will lead you to just the message He wants you to hear that day. Follow how God leads you and enjoy your spiritual journey with Him.

So, my friend, read, be encouraged, and comforted and listen close as He whispers into <u>your</u> heart.

And so, He whispered…

Precious One,

Slow down, relax, close out the noise in your head. Come, I have something for you. I want you to listen to the symphony of my heart. Let my Spirit draw you in. Reach for me, my child.

Section 1

Journey Into His Heart

He said, "Write It Down"

"My Child,

Be at peace and enjoy the ride. I will show you many wonderous things as you study My Word and seek to know me better. Pray often for I am listening. I care about all that concerns you. I love it when you come to me. Not only do I see into your heart, but you get a chance to glimpse into mine.

I want you to know my heart and the great love that I have for you. As you encounter my love, you will want to draw closer, and your heart will begin to resemble mine as we spend time in this holy communion.

While your heart is open to me, I will speak to you. What you hear in your heart comes from My heart. Listen and then write it down. In the days to come, you will read over these words and be blessed and comforted.

Write to preserve what I have said to you. Days will come when your heart will be burdened with the cares of the world and my voice will seem muffled. The words you have written will reconnect us...when you need me the most."

A significant change began to take place in my spiritual life when I started to write the thoughts and ideas God was placing in my spirit. Before journaling, I would get up from my prayer time and would soon forget what he said. I'm glad he told me to write it down. Many times, I have gone back and been blessed again by words from the past.

***Jeremiah 29:12-13* (NLT)** *In those days when you pray, I will listen. If you look for me wholeheartedly, you will find me.*

***Revelation 1:19* (NLT)** *Write down what you have seen — both the things that are now happening and the things that will happen.*

***Isaiah 30:8* (NLT)** *Now go and write down these words. Write them in a book. They will stand until the end of time as a witness.*

***1 Corinthians 2:10* (TPT)** *But God now unveils these profound realities to us by the Spirit. Yes, He reveals to us His inmost heart and deepest mysteries through the Holy Spirit, who constantly explores all things.*

"Lord, help me make a difference."

That was my prayer, and I heard Him Whisper…

"My Child,

As you begin to glimpse at the greatness of my love for you, you will see the possibilities that lie ahead. Yet, even so, you are only seeing through a pinhole with squinted eyes. What I have planned for you is way beyond your imagination!

Wider vision comes through time spent in My presence. Faith in that vision comes from time spent in My Word…attending the school of the Holy Spirit.

You will learn and you will move forward in knowledge and power as I lead you. I will walk with you and direct you in the way I want you to go. Stay close. When I turn, turn with me. If you pay attention, you will sense my guidance. You will note peace, favor, and protection.

My hand is upon your back, my child, resting just below your neck so that I can gently turn your head to see what I need you to see and move you where I need you to go. And…you will make a difference. Every child of mine has a heavenly purpose. I have begun a good work in you, and I am faithful to see it to completion."

Isaiah 55:8 (NLT) *"My thoughts are nothing like your thoughts," says the Lord, "And my ways are far beyond anything you could imagine."*

Philippians 1:6 (NLT) *And I am certain that God, who began the good work within you, will continue his work until it is finally finished on the day when Christ Jesus returns.*

1 John 2:27 (NLT) *But you have received the Holy Spirit, and he lives within you, so you don't need anyone to teach you what is true. For the Spirit teaches you everything you need to know, and what he teaches is true — it is not a lie. So just as he has taught you, remain in fellowship with Christ.*

And I Heard Him Whisper…
DRAGON SLAYER!

"Brave Warrior,

You long to make a difference in this world but doubt your abilities. Don't look at what you can't do, look at what I can do through you.

There is much to come in your journey with me, but during this time I am preparing you. Stay close to me and soak in my Word. Build your faith and learn to listen. Strength and knowledge follow time spent with Me.

I know the desire of your heart is to win souls and "slay dragons." I am the one who gave you those desires. Walk with Me and believe as you wait. Victory is coming. Souls will be saved, and the enemy will fall!"

When I heard the Lord say this to me, I thought, "He gets me!" He knows that I have self-doubts. He also knows that I sometimes get "fired-up" and want to jump ahead of him. I am so glad that through the Holy Spirit, he keeps me in balance…most of the time.

***2nd Timothy 3:16-17* (NLT)** *All Scripture is inspired by God and is useful to teach us what is true and to make us realize what is wrong in our lives. It corrects us when we are wrong and teaches us to do what is right. God uses it to prepare and equip his people to do every good work.*

***Ephesians 6:10* (NLT)** *Finally, be strong in the Lord and in his mighty power. Put on all of God's armor so that you will be able to stand firm against all strategies of the devil.*

***Revelation 12:9* (TPT)** *So the great dragon was thrown down once and for all. He was the serpent, the ancient snake called the devil, and Satan, who deceives the whole earth. He was cast down into the earth and his angels along with him.*

And I Heard Him Whisper…
OPEN THE TREASURE BOX

"Child of mine,

Let your heart be lifted into praise. The words I most long to hear from you, that delight me the most, are when you say, "I love you" ("I love you Papa, I love you Jesus"). And when you say, "Thank You". A grateful heart is the most fragrant gift of worship.

So, sit with Me and allow the Holy Spirit to remind you of things I have said to you and things I have done for you. Let your spirit flow with mine to sweet memories of rescue, provision, favor, and grace.

Open that treasure box of memories in your heart. You will find yourself overtaken in gratitude and enamored with the One who loves you so much! Praise will flow naturally, and blessings will flow out of praise."

***Psalms 103:2* (NLT)** *Let all that I am praise the Lord; may I never forget the good things he does for me.*

***Psalm 100:4-5* (NLT)** *Enter His gates with thanksgiving; go into his courts with praise. Give thanks to him and praise his name. For the Lord is good. His unfailing love continues forever, and his faithfulness continues to each generation.*

***John 14:26* (TPT)** *"But when the Father sends the Spirit of Holiness, the one like me who sets you free, he will teach you all things in my name. And he will inspire you to remember every word that I've told you."*

And I Heard Him Whisper…
WHY, GOD, WHY?

Why? Have you ever asked God that question?

In my experience and from what I have learned from the Bible, here is the answer. God is God and we are not!

His ways are far above ours. He sees the beginning to the end. We may not understand everything that is going on in this world, but one day we will.

God is in control. He is working His plan. God's will shall be done on earth as it is in Heaven.

So, you may ask, "What is God's will for us?" It is for good and not evil. It is for peace and not disaster. He promises us a future and hope. God is faithful!

So how should we respond to this world's troubles? Doubts count for nothing. Anger counts for nothing. Fear counts for nothing. Don't waste your time and emotions for nothing. Pray that God's will shall be done!

Trust Him. Don't question the one who gave His only begotten Son to save us. Trust in His amazing grace and love for us.

Romans 11:33 (NLT) *Oh, how great are God's riches and wisdom and knowledge! How impossible it is for us to understand his decisions and his ways!*

Isaiah 55:9 (NLT) *"For as the heavens are higher than the earth, so are my ways higher than your ways, and my thoughts than your thoughts."*

Jeremiah 29:11 (NLT) *"For I know the plans I have for you," declares the Lord, "Plans to prosper you and not to harm you, plans to give you hope and a future."*

Luke 11:2 (NLT) *And He (Jesus) said unto them, "When you pray, say, Our Father which art in Heaven, hallowed be thy name. Thy kingdom come. Thy will be done on earth as it is in Heaven..."*

And I Heard Him Whisper…
DREAM WITH ME

"My child,

Dream with me. Open your eyes to see what I desire for your future. Don't be afraid to wish for good things. Just turn those wishes into prayer. When you desire things that will bless you, my answer is already "Yes". I love you!

Don't feel guilty for desiring what is good, for I give you those desires. If a desire you have is not good for you, you will know in your spirit and you will be uncomfortable in proceeding into that desire. Be attentive as I speak to you in this way.

But dream child! DREAM! I birth My dreams through you! Open your heart to receive the dreams that I have for you. My dreams for you are for good and for the good things you can do. My dream sees you healthy, purposeful, prosperous, and full of joy.

Dance with me in that joy. Walk with me in our joined purpose. And most important, pray your dreams, for as you verbalize them, they come true…My dreams for you come true".

This book is a dream come true for me. The dream seeds were planted in me back in high school by a very encouraging English teacher, Mrs. Brandewie. Even if only a handful of people ever read this book, I pray they are the ones Jesus intended it for. It is for his glory that I write it.

1 Corinthians 2:9 (NLT) *No eye has seen, no ear has heard, and no mind has imagined what God has prepared for those who love him.*

Philippians 2:13 (NLT) *For God is working in you, giving you the desire and the power to do what pleases him.*

1 Corinthians 2:10 (NLT) *But it was to us that God revealed these things by his Spirit. For his Spirit searches out everything and shows us God's deep secrets.*

And I Heard Him Whisper...
RUN WITH THE WIND!

"Servant of the Lord,

Press on in this race you run. Don't be discouraged. Look not at your failings, but at your victories. Every small victory adds to the final great victory. Take note of these. You will one day see the value of small steps taken in obedience when the whole picture is revealed to you.

Stay with me faithfully to the end. Though you may tire and see no visible results, have faith. I will revitalize you! However, it is not by your strength, but the power of the Holy Spirit in you, that success will come.

Worry not, for all that concerns you. Your family, your health and finances are taken care of. If you have given them into my care, I will not fail you.

I have prepared you and will continue to prepare you for the next step. The work I do in you has great purpose and significance in the Kingdom of God. Therefore, take a fresh breath and run my child! Run by the wind of the Holy Spirit and by the power of my love that is upon you."

Philippians 3:14 (NLT) *I press on to reach the end of the race and receive the heavenly prize for which God, through Christ Jesus, is calling us.*

Philippians 2:13 (TPT) *God will continually revitalize you, implanting within you the passion to do what pleases him.*

Zechariah 4:6 (ESV) *Not by might, nor by power, but by my Spirit, says the Lord of Hosts.*

Ephesians 3:20 (NLT) *Now all glory to God, who is able, through his mighty power at work within us, to accomplish infinitely more than we might ask or think.*

Time to Listen: It is God's desire to speak to all of his children. What do you hear God speaking to you? Have you ever just asked Him, "Lord, what would you like to say to me today?" Why not ask Him now? Don't worry, for his answer is always filled with love and encouragement.

Remember, Christ died for our sins. When our Father looks at us, it is through the blood of Jesus. He sees a precious son or daughter who, because of Jesus, is washed clean of all sin.

So go ahead, ask Him, and then listen with your heart. Write his response here so you can look back on it later. You will be blessed.

_____

_____

_____

_____

_____

_____

_____

_____

_____

_____

For the Holy Spirit makes God's fatherhood real to us as he whispers into our innermost being, "You are God's beloved child!" (Romans 8:16 TPT)

SECTION 2

UNDER HIS WINGS

SOMEONE IS WATCHING

You do good things, because as a child of God, that is who you are. You were created in His image. You pray, make the right choices, work hard, and offer acts of kindness, and yet, your life seems to go unnoticed. In fact, unless you mess up, you feel a bit invisible. The truth is someone is watching you. Someone does notice.

Psalm 33:13-15 says, *"The Lord looks over us from where He rules in heaven. Gazing into every heart from His lofty dwelling place, He observes all the people of the earth."*

You are not just a random human being walking on the face of this earth. You are a child of God. The Holy Spirit living inside of you is proof that you are His child.

"All who declare that Jesus is the Son of God have God living in them, and they live in God. We know how much God loves us, and we have put our trust in his love." (1 John 4:15-16)

So, live each day for an audience of One, knowing that God sees you, he knows you and he loves you.

Feel like nobody sees you? God does.

CAST YOUR CARES

Prayer is a very important part of a Christian's life. However, praying also requires faith, faith in Jesus and what He did for us through his shed blood and faith in God's Word and his faithfulness to perform it.

I heard Him whisper...

"My Beloved,

Keep studying My Word. Keep seeking my face. I have longed for this from you. Don't be distracted by this life and its problems, pains, sorrows, and disappointments. What goes on around you can change quickly. My Word does not change, ever! My heart toward you is always the same; I want you healed, healthy, happy, and blessed.

Cast your cares on Me. Don't stew and worry. Just keep moving forward knowing that what you give to me in prayer, I will take care of.

You are on a new path now. My plan for your life is for good. No evil that comes against you will succeed. You must believe me. Ignore any attack from the enemy and know that I have already taken care of it. Know that my angels are "on guard" watching over you wherever you go."

Psalm 119:105 (NLT) *Your word is a lamp to guide my feet and a light for my path.*

Psalm 91:11 (NLT) *For he will order his angels to protect you wherever you go.*

1 Peter 5:7 (TPT) *Pour out all your worries and stress upon him and leave them there, for he always tenderly cares for you.*

Isaiah 55:11 (ESV) *So shall my word be that goes out from my mouth; it shall not return to me empty, but it shall accomplish that which I purpose and shall succeed in the thing for which I sent it.*

And I Heard Him Whisper…

COME OUT OF THE SHADOWS

"Child of mine,

The worries of the world overshadow you. This should not be. Remember that even when your life is in the shadows, my light is still within you. My power, my love, my strength, all that you need is within you because I am in you. No troubles of today will change that. You are free to be without fear and anxiety.

Dark, fearful thoughts are Satan's way to steel your joy and shake your faith in me, but Child, know that I've got you. Open your Bible and remind yourself of My truth. Picture yourself and your family safe, taken care of, and sheltered under my wings. Get a good vision to replace the bad one. See things through My eyes…My Word.

In life you will have some trials and when you do, practice trust and patience and watch for me to work on your behalf. Expect it. I will always rescue you and work things for your good. I love you!

Let this truth shine light in your darkness and then let My light shine through you to others who also find themselves in the 'shadows'."

Under His Wings

***2 Corinthians* 3:17 (NLT)** *For the Lord is the Spirit, and wherever the Spirit of the Lord is, there is freedom.*

***Romans* 8:28 (NLT)** *And we know that God causes everything to work together for the good of those who love God and are called according to his purpose for them.*

***2 Samuel* 22:29 (NLT)** *O Lord, you are my lamp. The Lord lights up my darkness.*

***Psalm* 91:3 (NLT)** *For He will rescue you from every trap and protect you from deadly disease. He will cover you with His feathers and shelter you under His wings.*

GIVE IT TO PAPA

"My Beloved,

Hold to your faith and believe in My Word. All is well, for I keep you. I walk before you and I stand behind you. Nothing will happen to you that I have not already made provision for. You are my child. My plan for you is for good and not evil, for health and not sickness, for prosperity not debt, for life not death.

Honor, acknowledge, and delight in me, and I will give you the desires of your heart. No weapon formed against you can ever prosper and you shall walk in favor that the world will never understand.

You will know your Father's eye is on you and His love is raining down upon you. You don't walk alone. You walk with Me in My Kingdom. I am writing your story. I am in control, not the world, not circumstances. I can change circumstances. What you let go of in prayer falls into My hands. Before it gets too heavy for you, give it to Papa."

Jeremiah 29:11 (NLT) *"For I know the plans I have for you," says the Lord. "They are plans for good and not for disaster, to give you a future and a hope."*

Psalm 139:5 (NLT) *You go before me and follow me. You place your hand of blessing on my head.*

Psalm 37:4 (NLT) *Take delight in the Lord, and he will give you your heart's desires.*

Psalm 72:6 (TPT) *Your favor will fall like rain upon our surrendered lives, like showers reviving the earth.*

And I Heard Him Whisper…
KID, I'VE GOT YOU!

"My Child,

You don't know what the future holds, not even the next hour, but I do. I am aware of it all and I hold you safely in my arms. Trust me, I will never let you fall.

Like everyone, you have concerns for what is going on in the world, and in your life. Just know your Father has it all in hand. You are loved and protected by the Creator of the Universe. So, you can throw fear back in the devil's face.

It blesses me when you trust in my love. I will protect those who cling to me in faith. When you call on me, I will answer. You, and those you love, will be safely held beyond the reach of the enemy.

So, bless me! Cast your cares and get back to listening to my heart and not the evil reports that the world offers. Don't let doubts and fears cloud your mind. With me, you can be strong and courageous, for you know who holds your future! Kid, I've got you!"

Psalms 55:22 (NLT) *Give your burdens to the Lord, and He will take care of you. He will not permit the godly to slip and fall.*

Psalm 91:15 (NLT) *When they call on me, I will answer; I will be with them in trouble. I will rescue them and honor them.*

Joshua 1:9 (NLT) *This is my command–be strong and courageous! Do not be afraid or discouraged. For the Lord your God is with you wherever you go.*

And I Heard Him Whisper...
THE SHAKING

"Brave Warrior,

Yes, there will be shaking, unexpected things that cause uncertainty in life. Do not be afraid when you see strange things happening in the world. You are wrapped up tight in my love. I will protect you and your loved ones because of your faithfulness.

Now is the time to set aside all distractions and serve the Lord with all your heart. Be ready when I call upon you to pray, to decree my words, or to assist another soul to find his or her way home. I will give you the knowledge and the words to say. Just listen, trust and act. I need your faith to come alive—to make a difference for all eternity. Don't be afraid. I am with you.

Stay close to me. You cannot be a branch that is separated from the vine. I am the life spirit that flows in and through you. With my help, there is nothing you can't do.

I have a specific purpose for you. Through you there will be more lambs to hear my voice, feel my love and spread my word. You see, this is no small thing I ask of you. It is significant. You will make a difference in the world and the lives of those you touch because you will be touching them with my heart."

Luke 10:3 (TPT) *Now, off you go! I am sending you out even though you feel as vulnerable as lambs going into a pack of wolves.*

Isaiah 41:10 (NLT) *Don't be afraid, for I am with you. Don't be discouraged, for I am your God. I will strengthen you and help you. I will hold you up with my victorious right hand.*

John 15:5 (NLT) *Yes, I am the vine; you are the branches. Those who remain in me, and I in them, will produce much fruit. For apart from me you can do nothing.*

And I Heard Him Whisper...

MY FATHER'S "TO DO LIST"

I heard Him whisper, *"My word to you today is from Psalm 121"* so, I proceeded to read that chapter, and He blessed me with this message:

"I myself will watch over you, I am always at your side to shelter you safely in My presence. I am protecting you from all danger both day and night. I will keep you from every form of evil or calamity as I continually watch over you.

You will be guarded by Me, your God and Father. You will be safe when you leave home, and you will return home safely. I will protect you now, and I'll protect you forevermore.

This is what I am faithful to do. It is my "to do list "concerning you. Now say what I have said about your safety and destroy any strongholds of fear that darken your soul. Make this your daily decree."

1. My God will watch over me.
2. God will always be with me.
3. He will shelter me from the heat of this world.
4. He will protect me from all danger, day, or night.
5. My God will keep me from Satan-driven calamities.
6. God will guard me Himself. I will be safe at home and when I go out.
7. My Heavenly Father will protect me now and forever!

2 Thessalonians 3:3 NLT *But the Lord is faithful; he will strengthen you and guard you from the evil one.*

Hebrews 10:23 TPT *So now wrap your heart tightly around the hope that lives within us, knowing that God always keeps his promises!*

Time to Listen: Sometimes when we are afraid, we just need to stop and listen to what the Holy Spirit is saying to us. God does not want us to be in fear. So many times, he has given me a word of comfort when I needed it. It will often be a scripture brought back to memory or just a soft whisper of love, letting me know he is there. He's got me!

Are you anxious about anything today? Ask the Lord for your word of comfort. Write it here. This will be one you will want to visit again the next time fear tries to rattle you.

_____

_____

_____

_____

_____

_____

_____

_____

_____

_____

_____

_____

For God has not given us a spirit of fear, but of power and love, and of a sound mind. (2nd Timothy 1:7 KJV)

Section 3

Our Father Calls

The Day He Called Me

There is a scripture, John 6:44, where Jesus says, *"No one can come to me unless the Father who sent me draws him."*

One special day God "drew me" and I was introduced to His Son, Jesus. I fell in love with the one who died for me and now He is my constant friend, my Savior, and so much more.

I usually write for an audience of believers like me, writing what I hear God speak into my heart, but today He said, **"Write to my lost child."**

I ask Him what He wanted to say to this child, and this is what I heard:

"To My lost child,

You may have forgotten me, but I will never forget you. I knew you in your mother's womb and have never left you. I have never ceased to love you. I have never stopped watching over you. I see you now. I see into your heart.

There is nothing in this whole wide world that can satisfy your longing heart. You look here, and run there, trying to fill the void, but nothing fits. There is only one thing that can quench the thirst inside of you.

I have a Son, and I want you to meet Him. His name is Jesus. I want you to ask Him to come into your life. I want you to take all of your dreams, all of your longings, all of your hurts, pains, mistakes, and sins and lay them at His feet. Then ask Him to pick them up and make something beautiful out of your life. If you will give Him your temporary, not so great life, He will give you eternal life in Heaven and a purpose-filled life here on earth.

If you do this, a new life will begin for you. Your old way of thinking will pass away, and all things will become new. The empty void that was inside of you will be filled with Jesus Himself and hope will unfold inside of you like a blossoming rose. Through Him, your eyes will be opened to see into My heart. You will begin to learn how great my love is for you.

So much awaits you, my child. If you trust in my love and follow where I lead, you will not be disappointed."

2 Corinthians 5:17 *Therefore, if anyone is in Christ, he is a new creation. The old has passed away; behold, the new has come.*

And I Heard Him Whisper…
STEP UP TO STEP OUT

"My Beloved,

What are you afraid of? What keeps you from going deeper into My love? I know you want to serve me, but I long for you to desire to be near me and to know me more intimately.

Trust me to gently carry you to higher ground. Your path that I have chosen for you is clear to me. I want to make it clear to you. Clarity comes through closeness. So, take that step up and come closer to me.

The enemy would have your life to be null and void. Not necessarily a bad person living an evil life, just a person living without passion. Passion comes from the heart. Let me be ablaze in your heart.

Run after My love! Delight in My Word so you will get a glimpse of that love. There is no fear in my love.

Child, step up into that love. Step up so you can step out!"

1 John 4:18 (NIV) *There is no fear in love. But perfect love drives out fear because fear has to do with punishment. The one who fears is not made perfect in love.*

Psalm 37:4 NIV *Take delight in the Lord, and he will give you the desires of your heart.*

Psalms 108:4 (TPT) *Your love is so extravagant, it reaches higher than the heavens! Your faithfulness is so astonishing, it stretches to the skies!*

And I Heard Him Whisper…
It's Morning

I have found that when I give God the first part of my day, He takes care of the rest of my day. When I spend time in prayer and reading and declaring His Word in the morning, my day just goes better. It may be an hour or maybe just 15 minutes, either way he honors my faithfulness.

This morning, I heard Him whisper into my heart,

"This is the morning of a new era. My children must be faithful to fill up the prayer bowls for there is much I want to do. I know your heart longs to see the wrong made right, to see my glory come, to see souls saved and bodies healed. Your heart holds the same desires as my heart.

So, child, speak your heart like never before! Pray fervently and often throughout this 'morning season' of this new era. My spirit will accompany yours and when you don't know what to pray let my Spirit put the words in your mouth.

The Holy Spirit will lead you to pray for things you may not have thought of on your own. Pay attention to names and circumstances that He may drop into your spirit. Seek and be open to His leading."

Romans 8:26 (TPT) *The Holy Spirit takes hold of us in our human frailty to empower us in our weakness. For example, at times we don't even know how to pray or know the best things to ask for. But the Holy Spirit rises up within us to super-intercede on our behalf, pleading to God with emotional sighs too deep for words.*

Hebrews 11:6 (TPT) *And without faith living within us it would be impossible to please God. For we come to God in faith knowing that he is real and that he rewards the faith of those who passionately seek him.*

Revelation 5:8 (NLT) *And when he took the scroll, the four living beings and the twenty-four elders fell down before the Lamb. Each one had a harp, and they held gold bowls filled with incense, which are the prayers of God's people.*

And I Heard Him Whisper…

YOUR PRAYERS MATTER!

"My Child,

Your prayers may seem small and insignificant, but I promise you, mighty things are happening in the heavenly realms because of what you speak in prayer.

Just as I chose Mary, a human girl, to birth Jesus into the world, I also enlist other chosen ones to "birth" my will into this earth through prayer and obedience. My eternal plan is not without human participation. Mary was willing to become "expectant" in my promise. If you pray in expectancy, holding my promise close to your heart as you wait in faith, you will see it come to life.

As My child, I have given you spiritual authority. Your prayers have power. Let my Holy Spirit direct you and carry my Word in your prayers with faith. Be pregnant with my promises for I am faithful to deliver."

A few years ago, God placed in me a desire to write a book that would reveal His amazing heart towards us. I sensed that He wanted to "birth" something through me, but oh, it seemed so daunting. However, His Word promises that his mighty power will work in us to accomplish more than we might think is possible. So, I prayed, "Here I am Lord, please have your mighty power work in me!"

Ephesians 3:20 (NLT) *Now all glory to God, who is able, through his mighty power at work within us, to accomplish infinitely more than we might ask or think.*

2 Thessalonians 3:1 (NLT) *Pray that the Lord's message will spread rapidly and be honored wherever it goes, just as when it came to you.*

Hebrews 10:23 (NLT) *Let us hold tightly without wavering to the hope we affirm, for God can be trusted to keep His promise.*

And I Heard Him Whisper…

EXCITING TIMES!

The scripture highlighted to me on this particular morning was Matthew 13:16. As I pondered its meaning and meditated upon it, I knew he wanted me to see and hear more than this short verse.

"Blessed are your eyes, because they see; and your ears, because they hear."

I heard Him whisper, but I also felt an excitement in the Holy Spirit as he said,

"If ever there were a time to listen closely and follow my instructions, it is now. Listen with your heart. Feel what I feel. Align with my will. There is no time to waste. How you use time matters. What you speak is vital.

You are on the right path, now move with an alert spirit. I will inspire and direct you if you will give yourself into My hands. There is revival, restoration and healing about to explode as the Holy Spirit moves through my people.

These are exciting times! Work hand in hand with me and you will see great things accomplished for the Kingdom of God. You have the power of my Name. You have the power of my Blood, and you have the power of my Spirit to guide you. Many sit just outside the door of salvation. Help them to open that door. Pray for them.

Intercede, Intercede, Intercede!"

Matthew 10:27 (NLT) *"What I tell you now in the darkness, shout abroad when daybreak comes. What I whisper in your ear, shout from the housetops for all to hear!"*

Ephesians 6:10 (TPT) *Be supernaturally infused with strength through your life-union with the Lord Jesus. Stand victorious with the force of his explosive power flowing in and through you.*

Revelation 3:20 (TPT) *"Behold, I'm standing at the door, knocking. If your heart is open to hear my voice and you open the door within, I will come in to you and feast with you, and you will feast with me."*

And I Heard Him Whisper…
LET THE DOMINOES FALL

"My Child,

I am able to do exceedingly abundantly above all you ask or think. You are not alone. My Holy Spirit lives in you. Imagine… you carry inside of you, all the power you need to accomplish great things in My name! I am at work in you and around you to see the Father's will come to pass.

I know you, child. Your heart wants what I want. Yet, you fear that you are not enough or that you will fail me. Listen, you plus Me is all you need. Lend your whole heart, mind, body, and emotions to my use. Together, we will see souls won and lives changed. Like dominoes, it will be a chain reaction of hearts falling into the Kingdom, one after another.

Don't hold back. You can't make a mistake. Move in my spirit and with my heart. I will lead you in the direction I want you to go. I will light up my Glory in you and there is no darkness that can extinguish it."

John 8:12 (TPT) *Then Jesus said, "I am light to the world and those who embrace me will experience life-giving light, and they will never walk in darkness."*

Acts 17:28 (ESV) *For in him we live and move and have our being...For we are indeed his offspring!*

John 1:5 (NLT) *The light shines in the darkness, and the darkness can never extinguish it.*

And I Heard Him Whisper…
BRING THE FIRE!

This word came to me in a dream. There were sick people all around and I wanted to help. Suddenly I saw a wagon full of fire! I knew it was Holy Spirit fire, so I instinctively grabbed the handle and pulled it as I heard Him say, *"Bring the Fire!"*

It takes the fire of God to bring healing in mass doses. There are so many that need this healing. If we attempt to heal this world on our own, we will fail. We need the Heavenly Fire of Holy Spirit.

So, as we go out into this world not knowing what or whom we may encounter, we must be ready and equipped with Holy Spirit Fire. If we are ready and equipped through prayer and the Word, God will place those in front of us who need this healing fire. Whether it be for sickness in the body, the heart, or the soul, He is calling us to *"Bring the Fire!"*

Matthew 3:11 (NLT) *He will baptize you with the Holy Spirit and with fire.*

John 3:6 (NLT) *Humans can reproduce only human life, but the Holy Spirit gives birth to spiritual life.*

Acts 1:8 (NLT) *But you will receive power when the Holy Spirit comes upon you. And you will be my witnesses, telling people about me everywhere...*

Acts 2:3 (NLT) *Then what looked like flames or tongues of fire appeared and settled on each of them.*

Time to Listen: Sometimes the Holy Spirit will speak to us about another person, someone who needs our prayers. We may know what that person needs, or we may not. Whenever I hear a person's name dropped into my heart, and I recognize it as the voice of God, I immediately pray for that person. If I do not know what to pray, I let the Holy Spirit guide me in a loving, caring, "God meet their need" kind of prayer. We don't have to know all the details.

Who is God calling you to pray for today? Who needs the fire of the Holy Spirit brought into their situation today? Let the Holy Spirit lead you and write that prayer here.

_____

_____

_____

_____

_____

_____

_____

_____

_____

_____

_____

I urge you, first of all, to pray for all people. Ask God to help them; intercede on their behalf and give thanks for them. (1 Timothy 2:1 NLT)

Section 4

You Will Know It Is Me

And I Heard Him Whisper…

THE FOOT WASHING

Artwork by Brittany Mikolajewski

He gave me just two words, yet those two words…WOW! Let me share with you a very special encounter I had with Jesus.

It was a Monday morning, and I was with my then seven-year-old granddaughter. She was spending the day with us. I had just painted her nails hot pink and bright blue, (her choice, not mine). While blowing on her nails she said, "Grandma, I want to do your feet."

At first, I laughed and protested, "You don't want to touch grandma's stinky feet!" It did not stop her. She continued to ask, and I continued to object. Then she came to me with a square plastic foot pan that she found in the back of the linen closet.

"Come on, Grandma", she begged. She was determined! So, because of the look in her eyes, I relented. It seemed <u>so</u> important to her.

I sat down on the lid of the toilet and she, in total delight, went to work. She filled the pan with warm water then grabbed the fragrant bubble bath from the side of the tub. From the cabinet she pulled out a towel and washcloth and ask, "Where is your lotion?" She was planning on giving me the *deluxe* treatment!

She knelt before me and gently lifted one foot at a time into the warm sudsy water. I sat looking down at her kneeling there holding my foot and wiping it with the washcloth. I was overcome by the tenderness of this foot washing and brought to tears.

I looked up to Jesus with spiritual eyes and I asked, "Lord, what is in this little girl's heart that would make her want to do this?" His answer was immediate, simple, and clear. He whispered, **"It's Me"**.

When she finished her task, I gave her a big hug, hugging Jesus at the same time. I will never forget this experience. It is a memory that I will treasure in my heart forever.

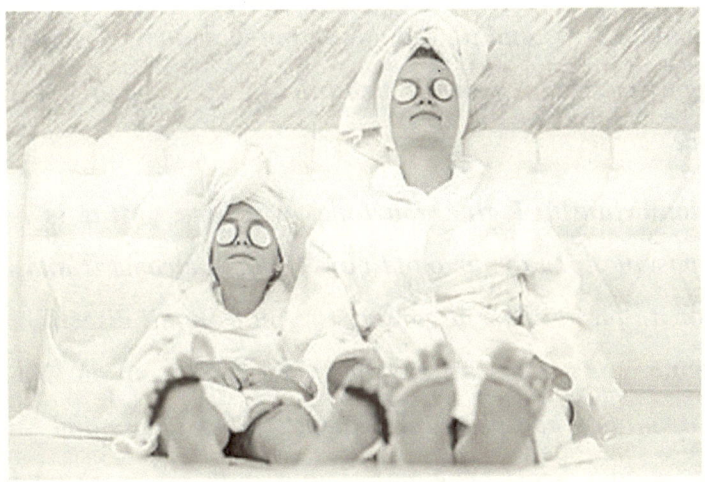

There is nothing so fun as an "at home spa day" with your granddaughter.

And I Heard Him Whisper...
SOAR HIGH WITH ME!

"My Child,

You wake and the weight of the world presses down on you. Thoughts of problems lay heavy on you. Fear and dread try to make a home in your heart. As you open your eyes each morning, block your heart and mind from these demons of woe.

Call out My Name! Cast off these demons who try to drag you down. I have redeemed you from the pit of despair. I have rescued you from darkness and placed you in my Kingdom of eternal light and <u>lightness</u>. Find yourself unburdened and weightless in my presence.

Most importantly, I give you love—My love. Mine is an all-encompassing love to surround you. If you welcome it and if you look for it, you will see it coming to you from all directions. You will know it is me no matter whose face I show up on. You will know it is me when pleasant thoughts cross your mind and joy sparks in your heart. You will know it is me working in the "temple" when you suddenly realize that the pain is gone, and the ache has subsided. It's love. It's me.

Reach up! Grab My hand! Come sit with Me. Be above all that troubles the world. See it from My perspective. Allow your spirit to soar high with Me. Picture soaring above the clouds as in an aircraft...The higher you fly, the smoother the ride."

Colossians 1:13 (NLT) *For he has rescued us from the kingdom of darkness and into the Kingdom of his dear Son.*

Matthew 11:28-30 (ESV) *Come to me, all who labor and are heavy laden, and I will give you rest. Take my yoke upon you, and learn from me, for I am gentle and lowly in heart, and you will find rest for your souls. For my yoke is easy, and my burden is light.*

1 Corinthians 6:19 (TPT) *Have you forgotten that your body is now the sacred temple of the Spirit of Holiness, who lives in you? You don't belong to yourself any longer, for the gift of God, the Holy Spirit, lives inside your sanctuary.*

And I Heard Him Whisper...
A God Encounter

This time it was just a little whisper, but an important reminder that we, as His body, are meant to care for one another and be thankful for one another.

He said to me,

"Be thankful for each child of God who comes into your life. They are there to bless you or for you to bless them. Whether you are the giver or the receiver, your Father in Heaven is glorified and my body on earth is strengthened. So always support and encourage those I send into your life. Be good to each other. You need each other."

I took this to mean that I should be looking for ways to bless my fellow believers <u>and be open to receiving</u>. This week someone unexpectedly wanted to pay my bill. I did not know this person, so I argued, "No, I can't let you do that!" She insisted that she wanted to do it and that all she wanted was that I "pay it forward." It was then I realized that God was in this moment.

She was instructed to give, and I was instructed to receive, and God was glorified through this transaction.

So, I thanked her for blessing me and promised I would definitely "pay it forward." We both went our separate ways knowing we had experienced a "God encounter" which never fails to bring joy.

We all have struggles to overcome. Kind words and actions offered in love can soothe where it hurts and give us courage to face whatever comes our way.

Colossians 3:12 (NLT) *Since God chose you to be the holy people he loves, you must clothe yourselves with tenderhearted mercy, kindness, humility, gentleness, and patience.*

Ephesians 5:20-21 (TPT) *Always give thanks to Father God for every person he brings into your life in the name of our Lord Jesus Christ. And out of your reverence for Christ be supportive of each other in love.*

Proverbs 16:24 (TPT) *Nothing is more appealing than speaking beautiful, life-giving words. For they release sweetness to our souls and inner healing to our spirits.*

SHAKEN TO AWAKEN!

Wow, so much is happening in the world. So much evil being exposed. A few minutes of news sends me running to my prayer closet. On this day, as I hit my knees, God reminded me that He is in control. He replaced the feelings of fear and dread with hope and excitement.

I heard Him whisper…

"My child, do you not sense My excitement? My plan of deliverance is in place. The blueprint forged in stone. This time in history has already been written.

My glory brings shaking, but do not fear the shaking. It is Holy Adrenaline. I shake to awake! Walk forward though you tremble. Hold on to me. You are safe. Remember the fire…the all-consuming fire that goes before you.

No matter what happens, I want you to know deep inside that I have you, and all will be well. All will be glorious!"

I declare, Love has come! God <u>is</u> at work. Our deliverance is at hand!

Psalms 18:2 (NLT) *The Lord is my rock, my fortress, and my savior; my God is my rock, in whom I find protection. He is my shield, the power that saves me, and my place of safety.*

Psalms 27:1 (NLT) *The Lord is my light and my salvation—so why should I be afraid? The Lord is my fortress, protecting me from danger, so why should I tremble?*

Zechariah 2:5 (ESV) *"And I will be to her a wall of fire all around," declares the Lord, "and I will be the glory in her midst."*

And I Heard Him Whisper...

YOU CARRY MY TORCH!

"Beloved,

This world is not enough to satisfy the human heart. All souls seek for something and that something is Me. Only the touch of My Spirit can fill the cold, empty place inside of them. You carry that touch. You carry my Spirit--the torch of my love.

When my Word pours forth from you, it will not return void. It will accomplish that for which I send it. You will be the vessel that carries my glory to the assigned designated "one". Pay attention, for I will place many of these "ones" before you.

I do not send you out alone, my Spirit will accompany your obedience. Speak as the Spirit leads you. Don't hold back. Do not quench the Spirit, but flow with Him. Do not let fear stop you. We are past that. The battle is full-on! I give you boldness, clarity and covering! Step up to the plate and my words will fill your mouth. Trust me. I will not disappoint you."

You Will Know It Is Me

Isaiah 55:11 (KJV) *So shall my word be that goes forth out of my mouth: it shall not return unto me void, but it shall accomplish that which I please, and it shall prosper in the thing whereto I sent it.*

I Thessalonians 5:19 (TPT) *Never restrain or put out the fire of the Holy Spirit.*

2 Timothy 1:7 (KJV) *For God hath not given us the spirit of fear; but of power, and of love and of a sound mind.*

And I Heard Him Whisper...
SAY THE WORDS

It occurred to me that fear is Satan's favorite tool to harass us. I hate fear! Fear is a lie from the biggest liar ever and should have no power over us. I know this, but it can still be a battle.

As fear tried to consume me (once again), I knew I had to choose faith over fear. I picked up my notebook of handwritten scriptures, saved for times like this. I needed to say the words–His Words.

The familiar words brought a calming effect as they always do. Faith was being restored as I declared His truth.

This time, however, I heard the Holy Spirit whisper into my being, *"I have a new one for you."*

I was excited to see what it was, that He wanted me to see. Picking up my newest Bible, which is the Passion Translation, I opened to the book of Romans. This is the scripture He led me to:

Romans 16:20: *"And the God of peace will swiftly pound Satan to a pulp under your feet! And the wonderful favor of our Lord Jesus will surround you."*

I love it! Pound! Pound! Pound! The Passion Translation is just so...so passionate! —as is God's love for us.

This verse, **Romans 16:20**, has now been penned into my notebook. I also checked it out in some of the other versions, and from each version, it is clear that God is fighting for us and has given us the victory!

KJV: And the God of peace shall bruise Satan under your feet shortly...

NLT: The God of peace will soon crush Satan under your feet...

MESSAGE BIBLE: ...Before you know it, the God of peace will come down on Satan with both feet, stomping him into the dirt! (I love this one too!)

LISTEN UP!

"Child,

You know my voice. Trust what you hear in your spirit. As I prompt you, take note. Listen up!

The Spirit is flowing, and revival is at hand. I need my children ready to respond to the inclinations I place in their heart.

You will recognize me in these moments... random thoughts of love and concern toward others suddenly becomes your personal assignment. You will know it is me. Be confident that I will back up the directions I give you.

Listen and obey quickly. Do the act of kindness. Speak the words of truth and encouragement. Pray with compassion. Bless as I direct.

My child, keep your ear close to my chest. Hear my heart and trust what you hear."

I recently heard this quote, "Delayed obedience is disobedience." Ouch! I never want to disobey God, but there have been times when He had to tell me to do something more than once. Either I was afraid to do what He was asking, or let myself get distracted, as if what he wanted me to do was not important. I realized, I was being a stubborn, disobedient child.

John 10:27 (NLT) *My sheep listen to my voice; I know them, and they follow me.*

Romans 8:14 (TPT) *The mature children of God are those who are moved by the impulses of the Holy Spirit.*

Deuteronomy 32:2 (NLT) *Let my words fall like rain on tender grass, like gentle showers on young plants I will proclaim the name of the Lord: How glorious is our God!*

Time to Listen: God is most likely to speak to us when we close out all distractions and make time for Him. When our bodies are active and our minds are filled with thoughts of the day and worries about tomorrow, God's voice can get muffled.

To truly connect and hear His voice, we must step away from this world for a little while and step into the Heavenly realm. The Bible tells us to enter his gates with thanksgiving and go into his courts with praise. I find that praise is always a good way to start.

If I have nothing in particular on my mind, I usually ask, "Lord, what's on your heart today?" Try it and see what he says.

_____

_____

_____

_____

_____

_____

_____

_____

_____

_____

My Loving God, the harp of my heart will praise you. Your faithful heart toward us will be the theme of my song. (Psalm 71:22 TPT)

SECTION 5

IMMERSED IN HIS PRESENCE

THE DANCE

I think most of us agree that life can be quite stressful at times. The news media is pushing doom, gloom, and fear. I personally, run from the news, but somehow it catches up to me and I have to hear about one more awful thing going on in the world.

Every day, for me, is a spiritual battle to stay in peace. But God is there for me and through His Word, prayer, and praise, I find my way back to faith.

Early in the summer of 2020, just a few months into the Covid Pandemic, I found myself extra fearful, anxious, and disappointed because there was no foreseeable end to it. I struggled for victory over this bout of anxiety, trying to wrestle faith over fear.

One evening during that summer, my husband left the house to run some errands, and I had some time to myself, but I chose not to spend it alone. I needed rescued. I needed Jesus!

Putting on my favorite worship music, I sat on the floor hoping to find Jesus. As the music moved me, I raised my arms (praising or begging, I'm not sure), and I opened the conversation simply saying, "Jesus".

He met me right there in my living room. As I confessed my lack of faith, my bad attitude, and my need for Him, His presence surrounded me. I began to feel my sad soul being lifted so I stood up just as an upbeat song began to play. My body swayed in praise with the song, and I fell deeper into worship. Praising the God who is bigger than all our troubles. The God whose faithful promises are our armor and protection and whose love endures forever!

There is power in our praise and joy began to fill my heart. My feet began to move, and I was in a heavenly place. I swayed and twirled and suddenly with my spiritual eyes, I could see Jesus dancing with me!

Immersed in His Presence

I could feel God smiling at me. I felt like a beautiful, little Ballerina dancing for her father—that is, until I caught a glimpse of myself in the mirror...then I felt kind of foolish. My joy turned to embarrassment.

But the Holy Spirit whispered this saving thought into my heart, ***"Girl, You Just Danced with Jesus!"***

"Yes, I did, and it was so awesome!" A glimpse of Glory! I changed from being fearful to joyful. I was refreshed and restored.

Just then, I heard the garage door opening. Hubby was home and my secret dance party was over. However, as my heart went back to Jesus, I heard him whisper, ***"Let's dance again sometime."***

...and we have.

And I Heard Him Whisper…
GLORY BE!

"Sit with me my child and let my glory pour into you. Your prayers do not go unheard or unnoticed. Your prayers are treasured by your Father and your faith shall be rewarded. I collect each of my children's prayers in a secret place, gathering and gathering until that day when they will be poured out and my glory shall flood your nation, and the world will see Whose you are.

I am bringing my glory to earth in ways and amounts not seen before. As my children drench in my presence, I am saying, "Glory Be!" There will be glory amassed in my people through My Spirit — world changing power carried in my earthen vessels. At the right time, the accumulated power will be released upon this earth.

My glory radiates miracle working power. My glory, released through my people will create supernatural breakthroughs. But, my child, you must sit with me and ask for this glory-power. It can only be transferred when our hearts are joined as one.

Ask and then repeat with me, "Glory Be, Glory Be" and it shall be."

Isaiah 43:7 (NLT) *Bring all who claim me as their God, for I have made them for my glory. It was I who created them.*

Romans 8:18 (TPT) *I am convinced that any suffering we endure is less than nothing compared to the magnitude of glory that is about to be unveiled within us.*

Psalms 24:7-8 (TPT) *So wake up, you living gateways. Lift up your heads, you doorways of eternity! Welcome the King of Glory, for he is about to come through you. You ask, "who is this King of Glory?" Yahweh, armed and ready for battle, Yahweh, invincible in every way!*

And I Heard Him Whisper...

"Open" in the Mind of Christ

"My Child,

You come to me, but your thoughts are all jumbled. You seek me but your spirit is all aflutter. Settle your spirit into mine.

Close your mind, and "open" in the mind of Christ. As on a computer, have only one screen open and focus on it — on Me. Click out of everything else.

Give me all of you for just a little while. I want to speak to you. You have been given the mind of Christ. When your spirit enters into mine, revelation begins and truths are revealed, and My will becomes clear.

I have dreams and desires that require your attention. I need for you to listen and do. It will be little things that I ask of you, but if you are obedient, little actions can be very significant in the scheme of My eternal plan.

I am looking for "doers". Will you be one of my doers?

What I ask will not be hard for I will give you the necessary ability. I will also give you the desire to do it. Our intentions will become one. My purpose will be fulfilled in your desire and in your doing. Just say yes."

1 Corinthians 2:16 (NLT) *For who can know the Lord's thoughts? …But we understand these things, for we have the mind of Christ.*

James 1:22 (ESV) *But be doers of the word, and not hearers only, deceiving yourselves.*

Philippians 2:13 (NLT) *For God is working in you, giving you the desire and the power to do what pleases Him.*

And I Heard Him Whisper...

SITTING WITH THE KING

"My Child,

I have seated you with my Son, Jesus, right next to My throne. You are surrounded by majesty, power, and the glory that is Me. There are hosts of angels, crowds of worshippers, beautiful music-- and there is you. Picture yourself there. Envision this truth.

Remain seated in Christ Jesus. He is before you and behind you. He surrounds you! While in your heavenly seat, you are wrapped in the total love and protection of your Savior. Nothing can touch you. No demon would dare come near!

Remember your special seat. I have assigned it to you. Your name is on it. Live from this privileged place."

1 Peter 3:22 (NLT) *Now Christ has gone to heaven. He is seated in the place of honor next to God, and all the angels and the authorities and powers accept his authority.*

Ephesians 2:6 (NLT) *For he raised us from the dead along with Christ and seated us with him in the heavenly realms because we are united with Christ Jesus.*

Isaiah 45:3 (NLT) *And I will give you treasures hidden in the darkness — secret riches. I will do this so that you may know that I am the Lord, the God of Israel, the one who calls you by name.*

The "Little Foxes"

"Child of Mine,

I am at work in you. I am personally tutoring you in my ways. And yes, I am cleansing your spirit so that our spirits, yours and mine, can meld together and work in unison. There is guilt that you should not carry, sorrows you must let go of, and pride that you are unaware of. These little "foxes" must be dealt with before your spirit can soar with mine.

Renew your spirit with My Word each day. As our spirits join together, your heart will change too. My love will manifest in you beyond the power of your own human heart. Your body, too, will manifest my presence in strength and energy. You will marvel at the difference.

So, stay close, child. Do not wonder from My presence. Stay under My wings where I can protect you and guide you."

Song of Songs 2:15 (TPT) *You must catch the troubling foxes, those sly little foxes that hinder our relationship. For they raid our budding vineyard of love to ruin what I've planted within you. Will you catch them and remove them for me? We will do it together.*

Ephesians 4:22-24 (ESV) *Put off your old self, which belongs to your former manner of life…and be renewed in the spirit of your minds, and put on the new self, created after the likeness of God in true righteousness and holiness.*

Psalms 91:4 (NLT) *He will cover you with his feathers and shelter you under his wings. His faithful promises are your armor and protection.*

And I Heard Him Whisper…

THE WHIRLWIND!

"Beloved,

Close your eyes so you can see me. I stand before you. Turn around, I am behind you. Look to the left, I am there. Look to the right, I am there. My presence surrounds you and envelopes you — wraps you in my love.

Now, look inside you. Do you see the light? I am in you. All that I am, is in you. You have more strength than you are aware of.

You are in Me, and I am in you. Together, we are a whirlwind of power! We have the strength to tear down and destroy the towers and strongholds of the enemy. Greater is He that is in you, than he that is in the world.

Up until now, you have been a gentle breeze of my love, but now is the time to kick it up. Move in my power! Pray and declare my Word like never before!

Your faith in me creates the power. Your prayers energize it. Walk bravely into the darkness and activate the whirlwind!"

> **Psalms 144:2 (TPT)** *He's my shelter of love and my fortress of faith, who wraps himself around me as a secure shield. I hide myself in this one who subdues enemies before me.*

John 15:7 (TPT) *But if you live in life-union with me and if my words live powerfully within you — then you can ask whatever you desire, and it will be done.*

2 Corinthians 10:4 (ESV) *For the weapons of our warfare are not of the flesh but have divine power to destroy strongholds.*

John 8 12 (NLT) *"I am the light of the world. If you follow me, you won't have to walk in darkness, because you will have the light that leads to life."*

And I Heard Him Whisper…
DEEP, DEEP JOY

"Child of My Heart,

You are my delight. I look upon you and smile, for you are mine. I sing over you and watch you as you sleep. I will never leave your side. I love you so much. It is important that you know just how wide and deep my love is for you.

Stay awhile with me. Let your spiritual eyes gaze into my heart and don't hesitate to step in. Allow my heart to wrap around you, comfort and warm you. In this place you are lifted up, safe and free. There is no guilt, fear, or anxiety. Pain must cease. No enemy can enter here.

Be strengthened my child. Don't just lean on me, lean into me. Feel the fire ablaze there. That is my heart toward you. My desire for your healing, your stability, and your joy…deep, deep joy.

When you step out, and I know you must, take the fire with you. Continue to believe in the power of my love. It is in you now. Do not let the world extinguish it but use it to warm another heart and light another fire that will light the way to another and another and another…."

Zephaniah 3:17 (NLT) *For the Lord your God is living among you. He is a mighty savior. He will take delight in you with gladness. With his love, he will calm all your fears. He will rejoice over you with joyful songs.*

John 15:11 (ESV) *These things I have spoken to you, that my joy may be in you, and that your joy may be full.*

Psalm 3:3 (TPT) *But in the depths of my heart I truly know that you, Yahweh, have become my Shield; You take me and surround me with yourself. Your glory covers me continually. You lift high my head.*

Time to Listen: Have you ever felt, what I call, the "pull to ponder"? It is when your attention is drawn to something ordinary, and you suddenly realize how amazing God is. It could be a sunset, a baby, a butterfly or even an ant! Knowing that he created everything with such intricacy, my heart is called to ponder and exclaim the greatness of our God! I believe that this is God speaking to us through His creation. He wants us to know who he is.

Take a walk and see if He doesn't speak to you this way. Write about it here but also share it with someone.

_____

_____

_____

_____

_____

_____

_____

_____

_____

_____

I ponder all you have done, Lord, musing on all your miracles. (Psalm 77:12 TPT)

SECTION 6

BEAUTIFUL IN HIS EYES

BE BEAUTIFUL

As I sought the Lord for inspiration one morning, I heard Him whisper, *"Teach beauty."*

My thoughts ran to when I actually used to teach beauty, as a skincare and make-up consultant. It was my way of getting to be a stay-at-home mom when my kids were little.

I could create smokey eyes, fiery lips, and perfectly blended cheekbones. As exciting and fun as that sounds, I knew this was not what the Lord was referring to. He was speaking to me of inner beauty, not the external layers that we add on. I find that the older I get, the more important inner beauty becomes. The truth is, when God looks at us, we are already beautiful.

Way before we ever cleanse and exfoliate, or in other words, ask forgiveness and clean-up our act, He already loves us. He already wants us. He already gave His Son to die for us so that we could be with Him for eternity in Heaven.

When we accept this truth of His love for us, when we believe that Jesus really did die for us, something beautiful happens. God comes to reside inside of us through His Holy Spirit. We have a direct internal connection to the God of the Universe — our loving Father.

There is nothing more beautiful than a surrendered heart. His light comes into us and shines forth from us. We glow! His light within us is true and lasting beauty at any age.

1 Peter 3:3-4 (NLT) *Don't be concerned about the outward beauty of fancy hairstyles, expensive jewelry, or beautiful clothes. You should clothe yourselves instead with the beauty that comes from within, the unfading beauty of a gentle and quiet spirit, which is so precious to God.*

Romans 5:8 (ESV) *But God shows his love for us in that while we were still sinners, Christ Died for us.*

Romans 10:9-10 (ESV) *If you confess with your mouth that Jesus is Lord and believe in your heart that God raised him from the dead, you will be saved.*

Blessed and Highly Favored

"My Child,

You are blessed and highly favored. You are mine! You are loved and cherished and watched over like a mother eagle hovers over her nest.

You are protected with my shield of love and my army of angels are at your disposal — ready, prepared and available to you.

You are <u>My</u> child, not just any child. My eyes do not leave you. My hopes and dreams for you are beyond your imagination. I will not let the evil one steal your future. Fear not little one, your Daddy is watching!

I hold you and you will not fall. You will not drop from my arms. Live in joy, knowing everything is going to be alright — better than alright. Trust me."

Psalm 5:12 (TPT) *Lord, how wonderfully you bless the righteous. Your favor wraps around each one and covers them under your canopy of kindness and joy.*

1 Peter 3:12 (TPT) *For the eyes of the Lord Yahweh rest upon the godly, and His heart responds to their prayers.*

1 Corinthians 2:9 (NLT) *…No eye has seen, no ear has heard, and no mind has imagined what God has prepared for those who love him.*

And I Heard Him Whisper...
WHAT DO YOU THINK?

"My Child,

Take note of what you think about. What preoccupies your mind? What is it that pushes My presence out of the room? What voice are you listening to?

Thoughts can be powerful. What you think about, you eventually talk about. What you hear yourself say, you end up believing. What you think, say, and believe, becomes your reality.

Be careful what you think and say about yourself. Speak what you want to happen. Rise above with your own confession. Bless yourself with good words.

The lies of Satan floating through your head are meant to trap you. Resist him! When you say what he says, you put yourself in agreement with his evil plan. Remember, his plan is to steal, kill and destroy.

Seek to stay in My presence and listen for My voice. I will speak truth to you. I came that you could have an abundant, good, and fruitful life. Stay close to me, Child.

Don't let those negative thoughts linger. Cast them down before they can escape from your mouth.

I love you so much. I know that the spiritual realm is a mystery to many, but it is not meant to be a secret to my children. Let My Spirit teach you and help you daily as you navigate My Kingdom.

I am with you. I do not take my eyes off of you. Do not take your eyes off of me."

Proverbs 23:7 (AMPC) *As a man thinks in his heart, so is he.*

Proverbs 18:20-21 (MSG) *Words satisfy the mind as much as fruit does the stomach; good talk is as gratifying as a good harvest. Words kill, words give life; they're either poison or fruit – you choose.*

2 Corinthians 10:5 (KJV) *…Casting down imaginations, and every high thing that exalts itself against the knowledge of God and bringing into captivity every thought to obedience to Christ.*

And I Heard Him Whisper…

WITHOUT SPOT OR WRINKLE

"I am coming for my Church—my Bride. My people who love Me and have a passion for righteousness. For those whose God is the Almighty! For those whose hearts are marked by the fire of Heaven! These are not perfect people, but those with surrendered hearts that have been made perfect through my blood.

These are hearts that fold smoothly into my Word, line for line and truth upon truth. Redeemed lives, living out my salvation and decreeing my Word without spot or wrinkle. They do not change my Word to satisfy the lust and laziness of the world, but boldly declare the truth of my Father!

They stand strong for both love and truth. His truth <u>is love</u>, a love beyond knowledge. Only those who have received this truth, accompanied by the fire from heaven, can know this love and understand.

Draw near to the fire of my Word. Drench yourself in truth so that what you decree is pure. Increase your flame to enlighten those deceived by darkness. It is not my will that anyone be left behind."

***Ephesians* 5:25-27 (NLT)** *...He gave up His life for her to make her holy and clean, washed by the cleansing of God's word. He did this to present her to himself as a glorious church without a spot or wrinkle or any other blemish. Instead, she will be holy and without fault.*

***Psalm* 96:13 (KJV)** *...for he cometh to judge the earth: He shall judge the world with righteousness, and the people with His truth.*

***Revelation* 22:17 (NLT)** *The Spirit and the bride say, "Come." Let anyone who hears this say, "Come." Let anyone who is thirsty come. Let anyone who desires drink freely from the water of life.*

MELT INTO HIS HEART

"Today my child, focus on compassion. Allow your heart to melt into mine. Open yourself up to feel what I feel. Let yourself be infused with love for lost and hurting people.

As I place names and faces into your mind, begin to pray earnestly for them. Pray from the bottom of your heart. When you go out, I will be with you. Let me smile through you, speak through you, hug through you.

My Spirit is given flesh and bone as you yield to my heart. You become a portal, a channel for my love to pass through to bless and change lives.

I am sending out my Spirit to draw my chosen ones to a new commitment of compassion and love for their neighbor. Join in and catch on to the wave. Flow with me as we gather in the "crop" of new family members. It is harvesting time for the Kingdom of God!"

Isaiah 55:9 (ESV) *For as the heavens are higher than the earth, so are my ways higher than your ways and my thoughts higher than your thoughts.*

Galatians 2:20 (NLT) *My old self has been crucified with Christ. It is no longer I who live, but Christ lives in me. So, I live in this earthly body by trusting in the Son of God, who loved me and gave himself for me.*

Matthew 9:36-37 (NLT) *When he saw the crowds, he had compassion on them because they were confused and helpless, like sheep without a shepherd. He said to his disciples, "The harvest is great, but the workers are few. So, pray to the Lord who is in charge of the harvest; ask him to send more workers into his fields."*

And I Heard Him Whisper…
STAND AND SHINE

"Continue to stand my child. Stand strong and tall on my Word. You are royalty. You have been called to spiritually rule your region as my ambassador speaking my words. I am in you, and you are in me. You do not stand alone, but you stand in my power.

You truly can do all things that I call you to do. Do not cower to an enemy that is so much weaker than you. Stand up! Stand strong. You have the authority in my Name to cast out demons. I have given it to you.

Immerse yourself in my Word and by the power of the Holy Spirit, walk in this light. War against the darkness with my Word and my love. The darkness is great, but my light destroys the darkness. When my children bring the light, the darkness will disappear. So, shine my child, SHINE!"

The more I study God's Word, the more I realize that we, as followers of Christ, are not meant to just be by-standers in this world. Merely being church goers, standing around waiting on Jesus to return is not what God intended for us. We are meant to step into the battle. Greater is the one who lives in us than he that is in the world. He placed His light and His power in us. We are his hands and feet and we carry His authority in the Name of Jesus! So, let's do it!

Ephesians 6:13-14 (NLT) *Therefore, put on every piece of God's armor so you will be able to resist the enemy in the time of evil. Then after the battle you will still be standing firm. Stand your ground, putting on the belt of truth and the body armor of God's righteousness.*

Ephesians 6:10 (TPT) *Be supernaturally infused with strength through your life-union with the Lord Jesus. Stand victorious with the force of his explosive power flowing in and through you.*

John 1:5 (NLT) *The light shines in the darkness, and the darkness can never extinguish it.*

And I Heard Him Whisper…
DITCH THE BASKET

"My Child,

When I first called you and your heart responded with a resounding "Yes!" I put a plan before you and placed my glory upon you.

It has been a journey for you. Though you have not always walked as closely to me as I would like, we have never been apart. I have always kept you near to me; always watching, protecting, and prompting you to higher ground with me.

I continue to place my glory upon you, to shine on those you encounter who are lost. Just like it did you, my glory shall "light up" one person at a time. This will happen as they are exposed to a life changed by grace…you.

Let the fire of my Holy Spirit burn bright and hot within you. Do not hide it. Do not let it cool. Fan the flames to reach out further and further. Walk and move in a fiery love of compassion for the lost.

Show them the way. "I am the way" and no one can have eternal life in Heaven without Me. You must share this truth. Unless they are told, how will they know? Everyone will have an eternity. The question is, where?

Let that thought break your heart like it does mine."

John 14:6 (NLT) *Jesus told him, "I am the way, the truth, and the life. No one can come to the Father except through me."*

2 Timothy 1:6 (ESV) *For this reason I remind you to fan into flame the gift of God, which is in you...*

Luke 11:33 (ESV) *No one after lighting a lamp puts it in a cellar or under a basket, but on a stand, so that those who enter may see the light.*

Time to Listen: God gave us all unique personalities and talents that brought us to where we are today. He set us on our path and each of us has a story. If your story contains the day that you met Jesus, and how he changed your life, then your story can change someone else's life. Your story is your testimony.

Ask Jesus to remind you of that day and ask him what he would have you share. Someone needs to hear it.

___

The Lord directs the steps of the godly. He delights in every detail of their lives. (Psalm 37:23 NLT)

Section 7

I Will Meet You in Your Praise

PRAISE IS A BEAUTIFUL THING

As a writer, I have so much respect for today's music makers, song writers and worship leaders. I am moved by the melodies and lyrics that come from the hearts of those who love Jesus. Those whose talents give glory to God and lift the spirits of all who are blessed to hear their holy offering.

In 2nd Kings 3:15-16, we're told of Elisha, a prophet of the Lord. When Elisha sought the Lord, he did so with music.

"Now bring me someone who can play the harp." The next verse says, *"While the harp was being played, the power of the Lord came upon Elisha."*

Worship music can indeed draw us closer to God, and there, we can receive power. The hand of God will work through us to do things we could never do on our own.

I never want to sit down to pray or write without first getting into alignment with Heaven. The only way for me to do that is by looking at the heart of God through worship. In doing so, I remind myself just how wonderful He is and how much He loves me.

Psalms100:4 says, *"Enter His gates with thanksgiving; go into His courts with praise. Give thanks to Him and praise His name."*

It is by beginning our prayers in this way, that we connect with God's heart. We are not just lobbing Him a random "softball prayer" hoping He will catch it and toss back what we want. No, it is when we seek His face instead of His hand, that we get the really good stuff—far more than we ask or expect.

The desire of God's heart is for us to know Him. You can't get to know someone without spending time with them. I encourage you to "linger longer" with our wonderful God. Give Him praise. Name what you are thankful for. Remind yourself just how awesome our God is. In turn, your faith is enlarged to hope higher, believe bigger and receive more abundantly.

He is the God of more. The Bible says that *"no mind has imagined what God has prepared for those who love Him"* (1Corinthians 2:9).

So put on some praise music and take time to love Him. *As you draw near to Him, He will draw near to you* (James 4:8). On the truth of His Word, I guarantee it!

And I Heard Him Whisper…
I WILL MEET YOU

And He whispered…

"I will meet you in your praise. When you seek me, I will be found. I do not hide from you, but you must seek me with your heart, not your mind.

Your thoughts are not my thoughts unless My Spirit deposits them there. The only way from my mind into yours is through your heart.

Fill your heart with Me and your heart will overflow into your mind and spill out to those around you. Your words will quench the dry places with living water flowing from my heart.

Drink of me. You must fill yourself with living water before you can pour it out. When my Word pours forth from you, my Spirit and glory will accompany your obedience. Don't hold back. Let the river flow!"

Isaiah 55:8 (NLT) *"My thoughts are nothing like your thoughts," says the Lord. "And my ways are far beyond anything you could imagine."*

Proverbs 8:17 (NLT) *I love all who love me. Those who search will surely find me.*

Isaiah 44:3 (ESV) *For I will pour water on the thirsty land, and streams on the dry ground; I will pour my Spirit upon your offspring, and my blessing on your descendants.*

John 7:38 (NLT) *"Anyone who believes in me may come and drink! For the Scriptures declare, 'Rivers of living water will flow from his heart.'"*

SING!

"My Child,

When the world is crashing in around you and you feel there is no hope…there is! Look up child for there is always hope. Believe it and declare it with your voice!

Like Paul and Silas, in the darkest of hours, you need to sing. Sing of my power. Sing of my glory. Sing of my love and faithfulness. When you sing in the darkness (before you see the light), you proclaim your faith in Me.

Faith moves mountains! When you sing, the darkness is not so dark, for you bring the light. You bring my earth-shaking power to the scene. The candle you hold becomes a fire and the fire an inferno. The fire that pushes back the darkness, is held by you, who is held by Me.

The darkness that the evil one has cast over you will be dispelled! Sing in the darkness and you will be calmed. You will know I am with you, and I too am singing…singing over you in delight!

The flame of My Spirit burns in your heart. Sing and let it out into the atmosphere and the fire will spread. Light will once again radiate over this land and into the world.

So, sing my child. Sing the darkness away and step into the Light of hope."

I Will Meet You in Your Praise

Acts 16:25-26 (NLT) *Around midnight Paul and Silas were praying and singing hymns to God, and the other prisoners were listening. Suddenly, there was a massive earthquake, and the prison was shaken to its foundations. All the doors immediately flew open, and the chains of every prisoner fell off!*

Zephaniah 3:17 (NLT) *For the Lord your God is living among you. He is a mighty savior. He will take delight in you with gladness. With His love, He will calm all your fears. He will rejoice over you with joyful songs.*

Ephesians 5:8 (NLT) *For once you were full of darkness, but now you have light from the Lord. So, live as people of light! For this light within you produces only what is good and right and true.*

And I Heard Him Whisper...
PRAISE IN YOUR PAIN

In my pain, I heard Him whisper...

"Let praise be your source of power and relief. Praise cost you nothing but your love. Yet, your praise can produce great freedom. It holds the demons at bay and lifts you to a higher place. So, offer up your pain to me as a sacrifice of praise.

Lay your pain upon my alter. Be reminded that I am the one who rescues you. With faith and thanksgiving, rejoice that you will see the hand of God move in your life. Give praise!

Yes, praise in your pain. It is an outward sign of your faith. You will witness the resurrection power that is in you by my Holy Spirit. You will be infused with strength and energy.

Do not let the deceiver take your thoughts to hopelessness. Look into My Word. Steady your mind with the hope found in my love.

Your healing has already been purchased. Do not let My sacrifice for you be in vain. Believe. Let me restore that which the enemy has tried to destroy. That which I have promised, I am faithful to complete. Give praise!"

Romans 8:11 (NLT) *The Spirit of God, who raised Jesus from the dead, lives in you. Ane just as God raised Christ Jesus from the dead, he will give life to your mortal bodies by this same Spirit living within you.*

Hebrews 13:15 (NLT) *Therefore, let us offer through Jesus a continual sacrifice of praise to God, proclaiming our allegiance to his name.*

Hebrews 10:23 (NLT) *Let us hold tightly without wavering to the hope we affirm, for God can be trusted to keep His promise.*

Psalms 34:1 (NLT) *I will praise the Lord at all times. I will constantly speak his praises.*

And I Heard Him Whisper...
STAND ON THE WORD!

"Brave Warrior,

Now is the time to stand strong. Stand on the Word — My Word! You know the words. Say them!

Greater is He who is in you than he that is in the world. No weapon formed against you can stand. God's Will overrides Satan's lies. My Word crushes his attempts to hurt you. You are more than a conqueror through Jesus who loves you!

Jesus has already defeated Satan. Declare, "The Blood of the Lamb!" That Blood is yours. Jesus gave it for you, so that in this world, you could be healed, whole, and powerful!

My Word spoken by my children — spoken by <u>you</u>, my child, brings victory."

Isaiah 54:17 (TPT) *"But I promise you, no weapon meant to hurt you will succeed, and you will refute every accusing word spoken against you. This promise is the inheritance of Yahweh's servants, and their vindication is from me," says Yahweh.*

Romans 8:37 (ESV) *No, in all these things we are more than conquerors through him who loved us.*

Revelation 12:11 (NLT) *And they have defeated him by the blood of the Lamb and by their testimony. And they did not love their lives so much that they were afraid to die.*

And I Heard Him Whisper...
JUST GOTTA PRAISE HIM!

I was created out of my Father's heart. His Spirit was with me in my mother's womb and has been watching over me all the days of my life.

He has been so good to me. Though my life has not always been perfect or easy, My Father has never left me. He's carried me through it all. He took the hard times and turned them around for my good.

Not only did He create me once, but then, He re-created me when He saved my soul. He made me new again, washing away all my past mistakes as He drew my heart to Jesus.

Through believing Jesus died for me on the cross, God became my Eternal Father. I was welcomed into the Kingdom of God forever! All I had to do was accept... and I did.

I am in no way a perfect person now, but when my Father looks at me, He does not see my sin, He sees where the blood of Jesus washed me clean. (Thank you, Jesus!!)

I can't say my life is easy now, but through Jesus, I am given strength to overcome. I know that I am not His only child, yet He makes me feel that special!

God is a good Father, and I cling to Him every second of my life. I never forget that He is "Almighty God, Creator of the Universe," but He is also my "Papa" who loves me.

2 Corinthians 5:21 (NLT) *For God made Christ, who never sinned, to be the offering for our sin, so that we could be made right with God through Christ.*

2 Corinthians 5:17 (NLT) *This means that anyone who belongs to Christ has become a new person. The old life is gone; a new life has begun!*

John 6:44 (NLT) *Jesus said, "For no one can come to me unless the Father who sent me draws them to me, and at the last day I will raise them up.*

And I Heard Him Whisper…

DANCING IN THE KITCHEN

"Child of Mine,

No matter the season you are going through, search out and find your joy. It is there. I put it in you. Come to Me and we will bring it to the surface together.

I relish your praise, but what I enjoy most is when your love is expressed in joy. A thankful heart, overcome with jubilation, is the greatest praise. When you dance for joy, even in the kitchen, I dance with you.

I love you so much! I want you to help others know of my love and about My joy. I crave connection with my children, my beloved…with you.

When your spirit joins mine, even for a short time, it is glorious! Take that spark of glory and fan it into a flame. My fire on you brings revelation to others. Fan it more and it brings miracles. Don't shy away from my fire. The world needs my fire, my light, my healing and yes, my joy.

Let's dance again soon."

Philippians 4:4 (TPT) *Be cheerful with joyous celebration in every season of life. Let your joy overflow!*

John 15:11 (NLT) *I have told you these things so that you will be filled with my joy. Yes, your joy will overflow!*

Luke 12:49 (TPT) *I have come to set the earth on fire. And how I long for every heart to be already ablaze with this fiery passion for God!*

Time to Listen: I want to praise God from the depths of my soul! Yet, I stumble over my inadequate words. I just can't express the magnitude of who He is. My heart is full, but my mind is blank. This is when I ask for the Holy Spirit to help me. He may plant words in my heart by leading me to a Psalm of David, or he may fill my mind with things I am thankful for. Either way, I think it is a request he likes to fill.

I would like to encourage you today to ask the Holy Spirit to help you praise our Lord. Pick up a pen and see what He has you write.

_____

_____

_____

_____

_____

_____

_____

_____

_____

_____

_____

Let all that I am Praise the Lord; may I never forget the good things he does for me. (Psalms 103:2 NLT)

Section 8

Warriors of the Kingdom

And I Heard Him Whisper...

BE A WARRIOR!

"Child of the Most High God!

I <u>was</u> the sacrificial Lamb, and I <u>am</u> the Lion of Judah! I am a warrior, and I am in you!

This is no time for my children to be "lukewarm." I need warriors. Will you be a warrior? I have given you the sword of the Spirit! My Word declared in your mouth can break the back of evil, pull-down strongholds and set the captives free! Use it!

Stand strong! Activate your armor! Remember the power that you wield. In my Name, I have given you authority over all principalities, powers, and dominions! Greater is He that is in you, than he that is in the world!

The angel armies listen to hear my word. Pray and declare, my warrior child, for the angels of the Lord await their marching orders."

In recent years, God has revealed to me just how important we are to His plan on earth. For years I have watched as evil has grown and infested every part of our culture. I thought there was nothing I could do about it, but God showed me differently. He wants us to partner with him through our prayers and decrees to defeat the darkness and replace it with His light. I'm all-in. I'm ready to see the evil stop. How about you?

Revelation 3:15-16 (NLT) *I know all the things you do, that you are neither hot nor cold. I wish that you were one or the other! But since you are like lukewarm water, neither hot nor cold, I will spit you out of my mouth!*

Jeremiah 1:9-10 (ESV) *"Behold, I have put my words in your mouth. See, I have set you this day over nations and over kingdoms, to pluck up and to break down, to destroy and to overthrow, to build and to plant."*

Ephesians 6:17 (NLT) *Put on salvation as your helmet, and take the sword of the Spirit, which is the word of God.*

Psalm 103:20 (TPT) *So bless the Lord, all his messengers of power (angels), for you are his mighty heroes who listen intently to the voice of his word to do it.*

AUTHORITY OF MY CHURCH

"My Warrior Child,

Stay the course of praying and declaring My Word. You, my church, have authority over this world. You carry my keys to lock and unlock. What you say will come to pass so be watchful of your words. Speak what I have spoken, not what the enemy is doing. The tides will turn.

Study my Word to learn of my ways. Seek to know me, to understand my love and my power. Learn what it means to be 'In Christ'. You are made in my image, and you are to reflect my glory on this earth. A reflection of Me is more powerful than anything the devil puts out there.

No one who seeks my light will be kept in the dark. In the light you will see what is ahead. You can move forward confidently and without fear. I am protecting you. Remember, your faith in me lights the wall of glory fire that surrounds you. You are not alone. In the midst of it all, I am with you!"

Ephesians 1:22-23 (NLT) *God has put all things under the authority of Christ and has made him head over all things for the benefit of the church. And the church is his body; it is made full and complete by Christ, who fills all things everywhere with himself.*

Luke 10:19 (NLT) *"Look I have given you authority over all the power of the enemy, and you can walk among snakes and scorpions and crush them. Nothing will injure you."*

Zechariah 2:5 (ESV) *"And I will be to her a wall of fire all around, declares the Lord, and I will be the glory in her midst!"*

Psalms 112:7-8 (NLT) *They do not fear bad news; they confidently trust the Lord to care for them. They are confident and fearless and can face their foes triumphantly.*

And I Heard Him Whisper...

FORBID THEM!

"My Child,

Let my glory fill your heart. Speak life over your family and nation. Change your perspective. See yourself with authority, for I have given you authority over all the power of the enemy.

You have the keys to lock and unlock. What you declare forbidden on earth is forbidden in heaven. Look at your TV or news source and when you see an evil deceiver, declare, "I forbid you to speak lies! I forbid you in Jesus' Name!" When you see an evil politician who defies the living God, declare, "I forbid you, in the Name of Jesus, to hold office!"

My child, you have cried out on your knees for change. Now stand up on My Word and declare what you want. Bind what is improper and unlawful. Loose what is good. You do not fight against flesh and blood; therefore, your weapons are spiritual and divinely powerful to pull down the strongholds of the enemy.

You are not helpless. I am in you! You are a divinely empowered warrior! Born for such a time as this. Stand now. You have your assignment!"

***Matthew 18:18-19* (NLT)** *"I tell you the truth, whatever you forbid on earth will be forbidden in heaven, and whatever you permit on earth will be permitted in heaven. I also tell you this: If two of you agree here on earth concerning anything you ask, my Father in heaven will do it for you."*

2 *Corinthians* 10:4 (NLT) *We are human, but we don't wage war as humans do. We use God's mighty weapons, not worldly weapons, to knock down the strongholds of human reasoning and to destroy false arguments.*

***Ephesians* 6:10 (NLT)** *Be strong in the Lord and in his mighty power! Put on all of God's armor so that you will be able to stand firm against all strategies of the devil.*

And I Heard Him Whisper...

STAND AND ROAR!

"My Child,

Don't forget in whose image you were created! I am the Lamb and the Lion, and both are in you.

When I call forth the lamb, listen and obey. Move gently with me in love. Share my warmth with those around you. Encourage, support, and uplift them in meekness and humility.

But my warrior child, when I call forth the lion, it is time to be bold! Time to declare who you are, in Me. You are a child of God! You sit with me in high places above all principalities, powers, and dominions. You are the head and not the tail. You have been given the authority to trample on demons! They are under your feet, so, **PUT YOUR FOOT DOWN!**

You are My voice. You are My hands and feet. Release the roar, warrior of the Lord. Be what the Lion of Judah intends you to be. It is time for my people to be warriors now, not sheep. So, stand and ROAR!"

Colossians 2: 9-10 (NLT) *For in Christ lives all the fullness of God in a human body. So, you also are complete through your union with Christ, who is the head over every ruler and authority.*

Deuteronomy 28:13 (ESV) *And the Lord will make you the head and not the tail, and you shall only go up and not down...*

Joshua 1:9 (NLT) *This is my command–be strong and courageous! Do not be afraid or discouraged. For the Lord your God is with you wherever you go.*

And I Heard Him Whisper…

SCORCH THEIR TAILS!

I was so outraged at yet another senseless school shooting. I'm sure you've felt the same.

I sat in a pool of sorrow and anger that left me feeling helpless. With such heaviness I turned wordlessly to Jesus. He heard my heart and said…

"Beloved, the enemy who comes to steal, kill, and destroy, still roams about looking for whom he can devour. His time is short, and he rages to exist. So, he strikes at My children.

The blow has been vicious. So much so, you feel the wind knocked out of you. The devil would have you feeling helpless, but you are not! My child, it is time to stand up and take a big breath, deeper than you ever have. Breathe in My power and exhale Fire!!

You are a force for good. It is time to rise up to fight the good fight once again! Do not waver. Do it now. Don't wait to release the power. Take a big deep breath. Fill your lungs with my Word. The Fire of My Word, spoken from the lips of a believer, can scorch the tails of demons and send them fleeing.

Rise up my warrior child! Be filled with my Holy Spirit! Do not fear. I am with you. My victorious Spirit that is within you, is greater than <u>any</u> demonic force coming against you. In Christ, you are an overcomer!

The devil's fate is already written. It was determined on the Cross and will soon be fulfilled. But since you must live in this world as the battle rages around you, remember that I have not left you defenseless. My Word is your weapon of warfare. Speak the fire!

1 Peter 5:8 (ESV) *Be sober-minded; be watchful. Your adversary the devil prowls around like a roaring lion, seeking someone to devour.*

1 John 4:4 (ESV) *Little children, you are from God and have overcome them, for he who is in you is greater than he who is in the world.*

Luke 10:19 (ESV) *Behold, I have given you authority to tread on serpents and scorpions, and over all the power of the enemy, and nothing shall hurt you.*

WEIRDER AND WEIRDER!

"My child,

Expect things to get weirder and weirder. This battle is spiritual. Your combatants (Satan and his cohorts) will try to silence and discourage you. They will try to pull, push, and frighten you into stepping back. Do not fear, I am with you!

As the battle intensifies, do not focus on the world, focus on me. I am in control. I can do "weird" better than they can. My power will be displayed. What the enemy intends for evil, I am turning around for good. Trust me, my child.

Stand strong! Activate your armor! Greater is He that is in you, than he that is in the world. Remember the power that you wield with your words. I have given you authority over all principalities, powers, and dominions. In the power of My Name, you will rise victorious!

Expect to also see my glory as it sweeps this earth through anointed vessels. Miracles will happen. People will be changed from death to life. Eyes will be opened, wounds will be healed, and the lame will walk — oh yes, they will dance!"

Isaiah 46:9 (NLT) *Remember the things I have done in the past. For I alone am God! I am God, and there is none like me.*

Luke 10:19 (NLT) *Look, I have given you authority over all the power of the enemy, and you can walk among snakes and scorpions and crush them. Nothing will injure you.*

Jeremiah 10:6 (TPT) *Yahweh, there is no God like you; you are unrivaled in your greatness and might! The Power of your name is so great!*

And I Heard Him Whisper…

HOLY OIL

"My Child,

This is no time for my children to be "lukewarm." I need warriors. Will you be a warrior? Will you speak My Words? Will you say what is right and rebuke what is wrong? My Word declared in your mouth destroys evil and tramples demons.

My Words, spoken through you, deposit oil on dry hearts. I am speaking of those who have been so influenced by the world that their hearts are hard, and their minds deceived. Wrong has been changed into right and right into wrong. But My Word cannot be changed. Heaven and earth shall pass away, but My Word stands firm.

Be not deceived by those who make wrong right, though it is disguised in just enough "love" to fool even some of my children. It is a trick of Satan to bring confusion.

You, my child, know true love and true compassion. It is not political, and it is not sin. True compassion fights for the good of others. Fight my warrior. Feel my compassion for those who have been deceived. Cover them with the Holy oil of my love in prayer. Share with them the Holy oil of My Word.

Truth will always be truth, and it is truth that will set people free."

Micah 6:7-8 (NLT) *Should we sacrifice our firstborn children to pay for our sins? No, O people, the Lord has told you what is good, and this is what He requires of you: to do what is right, to love mercy, and to walk humbly with your God.*

Deuteronomy 30:19 (NLT) *Today I have given you the choice between life and death, between blessings and curses. Now I call on Heaven and earth to witness the choice you make. Oh, that you would choose life, so that you and your descendants might live!*

John 10:10 (ESV) *The thief comes only to steal and kill and destroy. I came that they may have life and have it abundantly.*

Time to Listen: Sometimes you may find yourself feeling inadequate, unimportant and maybe unloved. However, that is not what God says about you. Today I am going to give you some scriptures—His Words, that will describe who He says you are.

He made you his own child. (2nd Corinthians 6:18). He created every wonderful intricate part of you (Psalms 139:13). He gave you a purpose, and he calls you, his masterpiece! (Ephesians 2:10)

Look up these scriptures and write the one that speaks to your heart the most. Maybe he will show you another one. There are many. Listen and follow his lead.

_____

_____

_____

_____

_____

_____

_____

_____

_____

_____

_____

_____

_____

SECTION 9

STRENGTH IN GOD'S LOVE

KEEP MOVING!

"My Child,

When every day seems like an uphill battle, a mountain too high for you to climb, don't stop, keep moving. No matter the circumstances and in spite of enemy attacks, keep moving. Though your mind is filled with negative thoughts and your heart overwhelmed in fear, keep moving.

Remember I have defeated this enemy who torments you. He has no power over you unless you let him. You are mine. You live in My Kingdom, redeemed from the curse for I have overcome this world (John 16:33).

Satan is a liar. Ignore him. Do not dwell on what he puts in your mind. If he says you are sick, act like a well person! March forward in courage and defiance right in his face. You are a child of the Most High God. By Jesus' stripes you are healed. Keep moving!

I am your God, and I am faithful to strengthen you and protect you from the evil one. Though he may trouble you, he cannot win if you put your faith in Me.

When the mountain in front of you is steep, and your feet are heavy and dragging, walk with Me. I will make your path straight. I will carry your burdens. Place your faith in Me, the one who has always loved you and always will. Let me strengthen you.

Now, place one foot in front of the other and keep moving!"

Habakkuk 3:19 (AMPC) *The Lord God is my Strength, my personal bravery, and my invincible army; He makes my feet like hinds' feet and will make me to walk (not to stand still in terror, but to walk) and make (spiritual) progress upon my high places (of trouble, suffering, or responsibility)!*

Proverbs 3:6 (AMPC) *In all your ways know, recognize, and acknowledge Him, and He will direct and make straight and plain your paths.*

2 Thessalonians 3:3 (TPT) *But the Lord Yahweh is always faithful to place you on a firm foundation and guard you from the Evil One.*

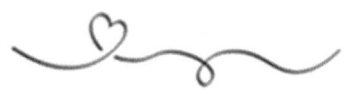

And I Heard Him Whisper…

PRAY, WAIT AND WATCH

"My Child,

Don't give up. Do not throw in the towel. I know that things seem too hard for you, but they are not. I am with you, though you find it hard to see me in this mess, I am actively working for your good. This shaking in your life, this uncertainty is necessary, for through it, you will discover true abundant living…if you will give your troubles to me.

You see, there are things that are simply out of your control. You cannot decide what another will think or do, any more than you can stop a world crisis. But you can hide yourself in Me. Tuck yourself safely under my arm and tell me about your fears and sorrows. I am here for you.

Nobody cares about you the way I do. Nobody loves you as much as I do, and you should not expect them to. There is no human love that compares to My love. In My love there is power. If you will embrace my love, walk in it, speak it, and trust me to take care of your problems, then I can change what needs to change…even the hearts of those around you.

There is no problem that is too big for me. Align yourself with this truth. Pray, wait, and watch as I move on your behalf. I am the God who makes wrong things right."

***Proverbs 1:33* (NLT)** *But all who listen to me will live in peace, untroubled by fear of harm.*

***Proverbs 3:5-6* (NLT)** *Trust in the Lord with all your heart; do not depend on your own understanding. Seek his will in all you do, and he will show you which path to take.*

***2 Samuel 22:40* (NLT)** *You have armed me with strength for the battle; you have subdued my enemies under my feet.*

And I Heard Him Whisper…

Yes, You Are Healed!

"My Child,

I know you are looking for words of hope that this trial you are going through will be over soon. Attacks from the enemy are not fun but look how it has brought you closer to Me…not what Satan intended (smile). So, continue to draw close to me and resist the enemy in My Name. He will have no power over you and have no choice but to flee. You'll be OK.

My plan for you is good, and yes, you are healed. The blood of Jesus took care of that. As you study and speak My Word, your faith will grow stronger, and your body will respond to the truth, "By Jesus stripes you were healed!" (Isaiah 53:5).

As with other sicknesses you have had, this ailment will pass in a relatively short time and then I will restore and strengthen you. You will find yourself set firmly in place with a renewed foundation of faith.

So, relax as I carry you across this battlefield. Rest assured, you are wrapped up in my promises and I will deliver you safely."

James 4:7 (NLT) *So humble yourselves before God. Resist the devil, and he will flee from you.*

Isaiah 53:5 (KJV) *But he was wounded for our transgressions, he was bruised for our iniquities: the chastisement of our peace was upon him; and with his stripes we are healed.*

1 Peter 5:10 (NLT) *In his kindness God called you to share in his eternal glory by means of Christ Jesus. So, after you have suffered a little while, he will restore, support, and strengthen you, and he will place you on a firm foundation.*

Hebrews 10:23 (TPT) *So now wrap your heart tightly around the hope that lives within us, knowing that God always keeps his promises!*

And I Heard Him Whisper...
You Shall Not Go Down!

"Beloved,

We are at work in you (Father, Son, and Holy Spirit) and the enemy is trying to stop what we are creating in you. He would seek to squelch what we have strategically placed in your heart. Don't let him!

When you look at yourself, do not look through the eyes of humans. Look through My eyes, the one who knows your future. This will bring you joy not fear, confidence not anxiety. There is no evil that shall befall you! I will hold you up! You shall not go down!

Father, Son, and Holy Spirit—your God, will hold you and carry you, delivering you into the works we have planned for you. Ride the wind of the Spirit. Speak the words we speak over you. Walk in the direction we lead you. We will keep your steps secure."

This was a very unusual message that God spoke into my spirit. The Trinity is a mystery of God that we accept on faith. Although we cannot fully understand how God can be three persons in one, as Christians, we interact with Him in all three ways: God our Father, Jesus our Savior, and Holy Spirit our Teacher and Comforter. Our wonderful God will meet us with whatever "face" we need.

Philippians 2:13 (NLT) *For God is working in you, giving you the desire and the power to do what pleases him.*

Ephesians 3:20 (TPT) *Never doubt God's mighty power to work in you and accomplish all this. He will achieve infinitely more than your greatest request, your most unbelievable dream. And exceed your wildest imagination! He will outdo them all, for his miraculous power constantly energizes you.*

Isaiah 41:10 (NLT) *Don't be afraid, for I am with you. Don't be discouraged, for I am your God. I will strengthen you and help you. I will hold you up with my victorious right hand.*

And I Heard Him Whisper…

ARMED AND READY FOR BATTLE

Sometimes God speaks to me in a visual way. As I sought the Lord's heart one day, He shared a visual message that was almost like watching an excerpt from a super-hero movie. I know, sounds weird, but it was awesome! He showed me the power that he desires to flow through us, his "royal warriors"!

"My Royal Warrior,

Open your heart and receive this vision: As you take my hand, we walk boldly in the face of the enemy. One courageous step at a time, thundering the ground as we walk. The angels of the Lord march behind us, swords raised! The enemy trembles.

As we walk forward, taking ground, I flash a wall of fire all around us and we push back the darkness. My glory is in the midst of it all and My glory is in <u>you</u>. We are unstoppable!

This I declare! The glory of the Lord shall cover the earth as my people march forth with me. When my glory is displayed through them, all the world will see my glory and know that I am the Lord.

Let my fire burn in your spirit. Let my glory spark in your eyes. Let my words pour forth from your mouth. The time is now. Victory is at hand."

Psalm 24:10 (TPT) *You ask, "Who is this King of Glory?" He is Yahweh, armed and ready for battle, the Mighty One, the invincible commander of heaven's hosts! Yes, He is the King of Glory!*

Zechariah 2:5 (ESV) *"And I will be to her a wall of fire all around," declares the Lord, "and I will be the glory in her midst."*

Psalm 97:3-4 (TPT) *All around him burns a blazing glory-fire consuming all his foes. When his lightning strikes, it lights up the world. People are wide-eyed as they tremble and shake.*

And I Heard Him Whisper...
WALK IN THE FIRE!

Friends,

God's plan is in place, and He will put you in place to fulfill your purpose. You need only to be willing. God will make you able.

He will provide you with all that is necessary to fulfill your mission. He will supply all your needs according to His riches in glory. (Philippians 4:19)

One day, as I cringed at the world news, I heard Him say to me, *"Walk in the Fire!"*

There is fire going on all around us in this world. It is not a time to sit down and coil back in fear. NO, we have a more powerful fire! The fire within us is greater than the fire that is around us!

And I heard Him whisper...

"Let the fire of My Holy Spirit burn bright and hot within you. Do not let it cool. Do not be distracted. Walk and move in a fiery love of compassion for the lost. Help them find their way. I am the Way, and no man can know the Father except through Me. Tell them.

Move in the fire. Warm cold hearts and light new fires. MY glory in you shall light up the darkness, one person, one soul at a time. Step out, so that I can step through. For you are a gate that I pass through into this world. Open up your gate."

Luke 3:16 (NLT) *...He will baptize you with the Holy Spirit and with fire.*

1 John 4:4 (TPT) *...for the One who is living in you is far greater than the one who is in the world.*

John 14:6 (ESV) *Jesus said to him, "I am the way, and the truth, and the life. No one comes to the Father except through me."*

Psalms 24:7-8 (NLT) *Open up, ancient gates! Open up ancient doors and let the King of glory enter. Who is the King of glory? The Lord, strong and mighty; the Lord, invincible in battle.*

And I Heard Him Whisper…

RIGHT HERE, RIGHT NOW!

"My Beloved,

Oh, how I want you to understand My love for you. There is so much I want to give you and so much I want to do through you.

You are not just a human being; you are a chosen vessel—a portal to carry my love into this world. But you are also my beloved whom I gave my life for and would do it again if it were necessary. Rest assured, the redemptive work is done and there is a glorious future in store for you.

When you gave me your heart, you entered into My Kingdom. You are a citizen of that Kingdom, right here, right now on earth!

Think about it. If I gave my life for you, wouldn't I also want to give you everything else you need? Wouldn't I protect my beloved? Wouldn't I want to bless you, comfort you, heal you? Wouldn't I want to see you smile from a gift I have given you? Of course, I would!

I do not want you to want for anything. Just ask me. I am your provider. Let me provide. All you have to do is believe. If you could understand the depth of my love, faith would come so much easier. My child, seek to know my love."

Romans 8:32 (NLT) *Since he did not spare even his own Son but gave him up for us all, won't he also give us everything else?*

Luke 17:21 (TPT) *The kingdom is not discovered in one place or another, for God's kingdom realm is already expanding within some of you.*

John 3:12 (NLT) *But if you don't believe me when I tell you about earthly things, how can you possibly believe if I tell you about heavenly things?*

And I Heard Him Whisper…

FIGHT THE GOOD FIGHT!

This is no time to sit it out. You were born for such a time as this. Step up to your calling. Get your dukes up and make a difference!

***1 Timothy 6:12* (NLT)** *Fight the good fight for true faith. Hold tightly to the eternal life to which God has called you, which you have declared so well before many witnesses.*

***Ephesians 6:14* (NLT)** *Stand your ground, putting on the belt of truth and the body armor of God's righteousness.*

***2 Corinthians10:3-4* (ESV)** *For though we walk in the flesh, we are not waging war according to the flesh. For the weapons of our warfare are not of the flesh but have divine power to destroy strongholds.*

***Ephesians 6:10* (TPT)** *Now my beloved ones, I have saved these most important truths for last: Be supernaturally infused with strength through your life-union with the Lord Jesus. Stand victorious with the force of his explosive power flowing in and through you.*

Time to Listen: Have you ever prayed and then gone off to figure it out yourself? You gave it to God and then took it back! I've done it myself, too many times. Instead, we must give him our problem totally. Put it in his hands, trust him, and leave it there.

When we choose to let God handle a situation, we surrender our way, to His way. Ask God if there is something you need to let go of. You may be holding on to something and not even realize it. See what He may have you write.

_____

_____

_____

_____

_____

_____

_____

_____

_____

_____

Then he said to the crowd, "If any of you wants to be my follower, you must give up your own way, take up your cross daily, and follow me." (Luke 9:23 NLT)

Section 10

Finding Peace and Joy

THE HAPPY PLACE

I guess I was born to be a "Lake Girl". Many happy days were spent with my parents at the lake, and then my husband and I got our own little lake place. I looked forward to each opportunity to be there. I called it "My Happy Place". In 2019, however, it was taken away.

At that time, we had moved my mother-in-law into our home. Her health was failing. Anyone who has ever been a caregiver for an elderly or sick person knows it can be hard. It can deplete you physically and emotionally.

There were a couple of times early that spring of 2019, I was able to escape to the lake for a day. I would relax and "re-boot" mentally and spiritually.

Then it happened. They called it the "perfect storm". It had not happened in 40 years, but the banks of the lake overflowed, and our little cottage was flooded. I was devastated! My "Happy Place" was gone.

As I was getting dressed one day, in my sadness, I was bemoaning my loss to God. That's when I heard Him whisper, *"Shouldn't I be your Happy Place?"* He spoke to my heart and reminded me that if I abide in Him, I will find my true peace and happiness.

I fell to my knees right there in my closet and asked for forgiveness for my self-pity and selfishness. His fresh waters of love and forgiveness flowed over me, and my soul was restored. He had led me to this place, and I was grateful.

Sometimes it takes a "shaking", or a flood, for us to see where we misplace our values. It is Jesus, not a place at the lake, that restores my soul. And, by the way, He made sure that our cottage was restored also. God is so good!

My Shepherd knows what I need before I even ask.

He leads me beside still waters and my soul is restored!

And I Heard Him Whisper...
NO PLACE FOR FEAR

"My Beloved,

I know that you are tired of being scared and living in fear of what's coming next. When you are in fear you find it hard to connect with me, because I am not found in fear. However, I am in you, and I will never leave you. But, for us to connect, you must exchange fear for faith.

There is no place for fear in My Kingdom, and there is no place for fear in my children. I have overcome the world for you! I bring you peace. Let my peace calm your heart and emotions.

Don't let the enemy think he is in charge. My child, I would not leave you in such a state. I am at work in you. Work with me. Declare that you are a triumphant warrior in Christ!

I want you to live victoriously and to walk in bold faith. Come up higher. Be an eagle! Rise up in me! Rise up to where you can hear my voice, feel my heartbeat, and truly possess the mind of Christ. In all the chaos, I want you to know in your deepest heart that I have you, and all will be well. All will be glorious!"

2 Timothy 1:7 (NLT) *For God has not given us a spirit of fear, but of power and love and a sound mind.*

Isaiah 41:10 (NLT) *Don't be afraid, for I am with you. Don't be discouraged, for I am your God, I will strengthen you and help you. I will hold you up with my victorious right hand.*

Isaiah 40:31 (NLT) *But those who trust in the Lord will find new strength. They will soar high on wings like eagles. They will run and not grow weary. They will walk and not faint.*

TAKE IT FOR GRANTED

"My Beloved,

Never forget the great love I have for you. You are my child, one of my forgiven ones — my forever ones. My love never ceases, it is eternal. Nothing shall ever separate you from my love. You can take it for granted... yes, take it for granted.

I know that sounds wrong to you but, think about it. Taking my love for granted means you believe in my love; you trust in it. This is what I want. Taking my love for granted will bring you peace. You will be able to accept my forgiveness when you fail. You will expect me to bless you even when you don't deserve it. Taking my love for granted can be summed up in one simple word — FAITH.

When you get in trouble, expect me to bail you out. When you are short on money, expect me to produce some. When you get sick, take it for granted that I will make you well again.

Your faith pleases me. You offer faith and I reward you with mercy and grace."

Finding Peace and Joy

Romans 8: 38 (NLT) *And I am convinced that nothing can ever separate us from God's love. Neither death nor life, neither angels nor demons, neither our fears for today nor our worries about tomorrow — not even the powers of hell can separate us from God's love.*

Lamentations 3:22-23, 25 (NLT) *The faithful love of the Lord never ends! His mercies never cease. Great is his faithfulness; his mercies begin afresh each morning…The Lord is good to those who depend on him, to those who search for him.*

Psalm 91:14-15 (NLT) *The Lord says, "I will rescue those who love me. I will protect those who trust in my name. When they call on me, I will answer; I will be with them in trouble, and I will rescue and honor them."*

And I Heard Him Whisper…

NEEDING TO BE HELD

"My Beloved,

On those days when your heart is weighted down by the world, your energy drained, your mind weary, and your spirit weak… let me carry you.

In your weakness I may seem far away, but my child I am always there with you. It just seems like I am not there because <u>you</u> ceased to communicate with me. But I know your heart. I remember the days we talked before and those to come. A Father understands that His child does not always feel like talking and sometimes a child just needs to be held. I will hold you.

You can rest upon my grace and mercy when you need it. I will not hold it back. We will share many great victories together, I promise, but on days like this, the victory is in just getting through the day knowing I love you.

In life you will have days of strength, courage, and fiery faith, mixed in with days when you just need a break. Lay your head upon my chest and relax. Stay a while. Be strengthened and encouraged in the warmth of my love."

Jude 1:1-2 (MSG) *...writing to those loved by God the Father, called, and kept safe by Jesus Christ. Relax, everything's going to be all right; rest, everything's coming together; open your hearts, love is on the way!*

2 Corinthians 1:3 (NLT) *All praise to God, the Father of our Lord Jesus Christ. God is our merciful Father and the source of all comfort.*

Isaiah 46:4 (TPT) *Even as you grow old and your hair turns gray, I'll keep carrying you! I am your Maker and your Caregiver. I will carry you and be your Savior.*

And I Heard Him Whisper...
THERE'S A BETTER CHOICE

"My Beloved,

I hear you as you pray and it is good that you are coming to me, but you are missing something. Whenever you pray, no matter how deep the sorrow is, always pray with a thankful heart.

Step out of your anxiety and into my love. Let the Holy Spirit remind you of past blessings and answered prayers. This will expand your faith to move mountains. If you fill your mind with things you are thankful for, there won't be room for worry. Worry destroys faith. Worry overtakes your peace. As you wallow in worry you can't move forward. It is like you are sinking in quicksand. This is not what I want for you, my child.

Look up and be thankful for what I am about to do in answer to your prayer. Thankful thoughts lift you out of the mire and up to where faith can take hold of your heart. As faith envelopes you, peace rushes in and calmness replaces strife. In this state of thankfulness and trust, you have life abundant, knowing that every need you'll ever have is already met. It is peace that passes understanding. It is abiding in me, not in your problem. A better choice."

John 10:10 (ESV) *Jesus said, "The thief comes only to steal and kill and destroy. I came that they may have life and have it abundantly."*

John 15:7 (NLT) *"If you remain in me and my words remain in you, you may ask for anything you want, and it will be granted."*

Philippians 4:6-7 (NLT) *Don't worry about anything; instead, pray about everything. Tell God what you need and thank him for all he has done. Then you will experience God's peace, which exceeds anything we can understand. His peace will guard your hearts and minds as you live in Christ Jesus.*

And I Heard Him Whisper…

MAINTAIN A GRATEFUL HEART

My friends,

I realize that peace and joy can sometimes be hard to attain and may seem impossible to you right now. Your pain is real and putting on a happy face doesn't quite masque it.

As I sought God, I heard Him whisper, **"Peace and joy are found in a grateful heart."**

I was led to Philippians 4:6-7. This scripture is significant to tapping into peace and joy in the midst of your struggle.

"…Pray about everything. Tell God what you need and **thank him for all he has done.** *(Acknowledge and be thankful for all that is good in your life.) Then (and here comes the promise), you will experience God's peace, which exceeds anything we can understand."*

I didn't say it would be easy, but I believe with all my heart that God's Word is true. We just need to activate it with our faith and the words we speak. Start now and say something you are thankful for, and then another, and another and another. Let your heart swell in gratitude and flush out all that magnifies your pain. Allow God's love to soothe and heal. All praise to our great physician!

Colossians 3:15 (NLT) *And let the peace that comes from Christ rule in your hearts. For as members of one body, you are called to live in peace. And always be thankful.*

Psalm 34:1 (TPT) *Lord! I'm bursting with joy over what you've done for me!*

1 Thessalonians 5:16-18 (ESV) *Rejoice always, pray without ceasing, give thanks in all circumstances; for this is the will of God in Christ Jesus for you.*

OUR OASIS

And so, He whispered…

"Precious One,

Slow down, relax, close out the noise in your head. Come, I have something for you. I want you to listen to the symphony of my heart. Let my Spirit draw you in. Reach for me, my child.

You will be lifted up and caressed in divine love. Experience the supernatural security as I hold you. Relax, I will not let you fall. Let me love you. Let me comfort you. Everything will be all right.

Hear the song of my heart and let all worries of the world fall away. It is just you and I alone in our oasis. I am glad that you have come to be with me. I rejoice when you seek me.

Remember this place, my love. Come again."

***Matthew* 11:28 (TPT)** *"Are you weary, carrying a heavy burden? Come to me. I will refresh your life, for I am your oasis."*

Time to Listen: One of the most precious gifts that God gave us, is our memory. I know, I know, there are memories we choose to forget. The ones that are painful. We all have them. I have found however, that God gives us what I call, "blessed forgetfulness" of things we don't need to think about.

There are memories, however, that bless me each time I think of them. Memories of the times that God rescued me from injury, healed me or the many times he brought me through something hard. Then I am reminded of just how good God is and how much he loves me.

Sit with the Holy Spirit for a few moments and ask him to remind you of a special time God came through for you.

_____

_____

_____

_____

_____

_____

_____

_____

I trust in your unfailing love. I will rejoice because you have rescued me. (Psalms 13:5 NLT)

Section 11

Rescued By the King!

WARRIOR DOWN

I was weak and shaky, but I mouthed the words, "I am a child of the Most High God!" It was all I could muster up to declare. A serious infection had invaded my lungs, and my heart rate was at a dangerous level. I was sick—sicker than I have ever been in my life.

Suddenly, my hospital room was swarming with doctors and nurses, and they rolled in a crash cart. I was informed that this team of medical professionals intended to stop and restart my heart! What?!!

They ran something through my IV that just slammed my body. I was aware of it all happening, but it was like a dream. Apparently, it worked, my heart rate came down and the paddles and crash cart were not needed.

Then, they were all gone, and I laid there alone in my thoughts. "What just happened?" I looked at the IVs running into my arm, felt the oxygen in my nose, and the tubes coming out of the side of my chest. I couldn't help but realize the thin layer between life and death, and I quietly asked Jesus, "Is this my time?"

Immediately this scripture came to me: *"Today I have given you the choice between life and death, between blessings and curses. Now I call on heaven and earth to witness the choice you make. Oh, that you would choose life, so that you and your descendants might live!"*

The verse is Deuteronomy 30:19, though I could not have told you that then, I only knew the words. But I knew that God was giving me a choice. I thought about heaven and an end to my suffering. There was no fear in that choice, just peace. Yet, I sensed that although God was merciful and OK with that choice, He impressed on my heart that he still had hope for my future on earth.

He had created me anew in Christ, and long ago, even before I was born, He planned good works for me to do. I still had a destiny to fulfill. I thought of my family that I love so much and realized that they had yet to see the full glory of God and what He wanted for their lives. I wanted more chances to reveal Him to them.

My decision was made. Although at that time, I only had breath in one lung, I knew it was breath God had given me and breath that I wanted to give for His glory. As long as there is breath in my lungs, it is His. I chose life, and I declared, *"It is not I that live, but Christ that lives in me!"* (Galatians 2:20)

Satan tried to take me out that day, but the Lord showed me that as a child of God in Christ, *"the enemy has no power over me."* (Matthew 16:18)

"I am in Christ and Christ is in me. Greater is He that is in me, than he that is in the world." (1John 4:4)

Then Came the Glorious Rescue!

Early the next morning as I prayed, the Holy Spirit gave me this amazing vision.

In my spirit, I saw Jesus in his flowing white robe. He was carrying my limp body across a dark and fiery battlefield. I sensed demons and Angels in hand-to-hand combat. Jesus moved quickly and with determination as He carried His wounded warrior forward to safety.

In the vision, I could see my short hair as my head dropped back over Jesus's arm. I was dressed as a princess warrior, but I had lost my helmet, and I had also dropped my sword. In that hospital, my mind had been darkened with fear, and I could no longer wield the sword of the Spirit to declare God's Word...I was too sick, just too sick.

Jesus promised never to leave us, and He would not leave me there in that defenseless condition. He is my Rescuer! Jesus scooped me up in his arms and ran me through the dark battlefield and brought me out safely into the light. Not only that, but in this vision, He set me on my feet, spun me around and set my feet to dancing! Even though my actual body was too weak to dance, I was dancing in my spirit, and I knew that one day soon, I would dance with Jesus again in my healed body.

As I danced in this vision, I saw that I was wearing a pretty red Christmas dress that sparkled in the light. I was overwhelmed with hope to be well by Christmas. Joy filled my heart as I thought of my family and our Christmas celebration.

That afternoon the doctor came in and said, "I'm seeing a lot of improvement! It looks like we can take the chest tubes out by tomorrow". Well, they did and that was that!

Three weeks later, on Christmas Eve before the others arrived, I stood in my kitchen. Having been rescued from that horrible battle and restored in strength, I began to cry tears of joy and gratitude. Music was playing softly, and I closed my eyes, and I heard Him whisper, *"Shall we dance?"*

I placed my hands in His, and just for a minute, a glorious minute, we danced. Jesus and me...the King and I. Thank you, my sweet Jesus!

And She's Back!

So now, forgetting those things past, I press forward to the future and my destiny for which God has called me. *"I am convinced that any suffering we endure is less than nothing compared to the magnitude of glory that is about to be unveiled within us!"* Romans 8:18 (TPT)

To the honor and glory of our King Jesus, my helmet is back in place, and I hold my sword high. God's "Princess Warrior" is back! All Glory to the King of Kings and Lord of Lords!

And I Heard Him Whisper…

IN CLOSING

The Funny Glass Clown

There is a piece of art glass sitting on my desk that I have never been able to part with. It's just a funny little 8" clown with big buttons, goofy hat, and curly yellow hair. It's not perfect. I once had to glue her hand back on and to be honest...she could use some cleaning.

I don't think of myself as clown-like, but somehow this clown represents me. I know, silly, but there is something about her pose that speaks to my heart.

She looks up to heaven as if looking into the face of her Father and she smiles. It's like she's feeling the radiance of His smile back upon her. She stretches her arms out in a "Here I am Lord" fashion, as if to say, "I'm yours. What would you have me do?" I have often taken this position myself.

This clown is not concerned if the people around her like her act. Though she hopes they do. She hopes she will brighten their day, because she knows that will make her Father happy. That is all that matters to her.

She is performing for an audience of One, The One who loves her and created her to be the silly little clown that she is.

The Lord reminded me of this scripture. Colossians 3:23 (ESV) *Whatever you do, work heartily, as for the Lord and not for men.*

I really hope you enjoyed this book. I pray that it brought you closer to Jesus and deeper into the heart of God, and a keener awareness of the Holy Spirit working in your life. Yet, it is not the applause of people that I seek. What I am looking for is that smile radiating from my Father upon my face, as I look back into His. That's all I want.

CLOSING PRAYER

Lord, you are so amazing! You created the earth and everything in it. You are mighty and majestic! You know all there is to know. There is no one greater than You. Who are we humans that you would even think of us. Yet you care so deeply for each of us, you call us your children.

You formed me in my mother's womb and gave me my place in the world and then…you came for me. Like the little lost sheep that I was, you found me. You turned my head so I could see you and then gathered me into the fold. You are the God who loves me and rescues me.

Jesus, from the first day I met you, I knew you wanted to speak to me. I could sense your Holy Spirit leading me and revealing things to me in the Bible. What used to confuse me became clear. Your love nurtured me along one baby step at a time until I was able to recognize your voice as you spoke into my heart. Your words were like love letters. I'm glad you told me to write them down.

Lord, your words have blessed me many times over as I have read and re-read them so many times. They are special messages of love that you so sweetly placed in my heart. Thank you for allowing me to share these words with others through this book. I believe it is a desire that you placed in my heart. I pray these words will be a blessing to those who read this book and that your Holy Spirit will accompany each copy that goes out.

Thank you, Jesus. I love you!

ABOUT THE AUTHOR

My name is Marcy Mikolajewski and Ohio is my home. I was born and raised here and can't imagine living anywhere else. I am married to a wonderful man and have two grown sons who each found beautiful wives. I am also blessed with two incredible grandkids. Life is good…God is so Good!

When I was 23, I met Jesus in a very personal way and invited Him into my heart. Wow, what a difference He makes! He has never left me, and I know he never will. He guides my steps in amazing ways.

The first thing He did was put me to work in a Christian ministry. It was office work with accounting, a little boring, but I got my first crack at writing when they asked me to produce their monthly newsletter.

I worked with this ministry for 11 years and it was rewarding, yet I longed to be a mom. Through a series of miracles, it finally happened—one son right after the other. Boom! I was a mom, and I was going to enjoy every moment.

I left my full-time job and began concentrating on a business I could run from home. I tried writing a book back then, but time would not allow. So, I sat that dream on the shelf of my heart for a later time.

Through the years, my life has taken different turns, but always centered around my family. I enjoyed being a full-time mom as well as being a business owner. First a skincare and vitamin consultant, then an antique dealer on eBay and finally when the kids were grown, I went back to work as an event-planner. I managed a banquet center working with Brides and helping companies plan their Christmas parties. A few years later I was hired by our local Chamber of Commerce. Working for the Chamber encompassed all kinds of event planning. That was fun, but then, along came my first grandchild and I wanted to take care of her. I wasn't going to miss the fun of being her "Mimi".

Oh, what joy! She was followed by her brother, and I never knew that 7 years could pass so quickly. Now they are in school and though I miss spending my days with them…this grandmother finally gets to write her book.

Like everyone, my life has been a journey of ups and downs, but God's Word and the Holy Spirit have been my guide through it all. In the years of raising my family, I tried to inspire my two boys to walk in God's purpose for their lives and to listen for His directions. I couldn't be prouder of the men they grew to be.

My husband, Joe, has been my rock and greatest encourager in all that I endeavor to do for the Lord. Whether it be leading Bible study, creating a web page for my blog or writing a book, he gives me space and time to do it. He has been invaluable in the editing of this book, and get this, he even cooks for me! Husbands just don't come any better!

My plans for the future include more writing. I am currently working on Volume 2 of "And I Heard Him Whisper…" and would like to write some Bible Studies. I know God's plans for me are for good, His Word said so, and I look forward to embracing each day as I walk with Jesus.

Contact Information:

Marcy Mikolajewski

And I Heard Him Whisper

www.andiheardhimwhisper.com

For information on Volume 2 of "And I Heard Him Whisper" use this QR code to reach my website. Also, you can sign up to receive my weekly blogs.

To purchase another copy of this book as a gift for someone, go to Amazon and search by title or my name. You can also find it through my website.

**Thank You for your purchase of
"And I Heard Him Whisper!"**

I hope you enjoyed this book and have been blessed by the words shared here. If so, perhaps you may want to purchase another book as a gift for a friend. Also, your positive review will help others to choose this book. Maybe they will be inspired and drawn closer to Jesus as they too take a peek into God's heart.

God Bless you!

Acknowledgement

I would like to thank my wonderful family and dear friends for their help and encouragement on this project. I could not have done it without them.

www.ingramcontent.com/pod-product-compliance
Lightning Source LLC
LaVergne TN
LVHW042252070526
838201LV00106B/304/J